TEACHER'S PET PUBLICATIONS

LITPLAN TEACHER PACK
for
Of Mice and Men
based on the book by
John Steinbeck

Written by
Mary B. Collins

© 1996 Teacher's Pet Publications
All Rights Reserved

This **Lit Plan** for John Steinbeck's
Of Mice and Men
has been brought to you by Teacher's Pet Publications, Inc.

Copyright Teacher's Pet Publications 1996
11504 Hammock Point
Berlin MD 21811

Only the student materials in this unit plan
such as worksheets, study questions, assignment sheets, and tests
may be reproduced multiple times for use in the purchaser's classroom.

For any additional copyright questions,
contact Teacher's Pet Publications.

www.tpet.com

TABLE OF CONTENTS - *Of Mice and Men*

Introduction	5
Unit Objectives	8
Reading Assignment Sheet	9
Unit Outline	10
Study Questions (Short Answer)	13
Quiz/Study Questions (Multiple Choice)	20
Pre-reading Vocabulary Worksheets	31
Lesson One (Introductory Lesson)	43
Nonfiction Assignment Sheet	49
Oral Reading Evaluation Form	50
Writing Assignment 1	44
Writing Assignment 2	56
Writing Assignment 3	66
Writing Evaluation Form	57
Vocabulary Review Activities	64
Extra Writing Assignments/Discussion ?s	59
Unit Review Activities	68
Unit Tests	71
Unit Resource Materials	97
Vocabulary Resource Materials	109

A FEW NOTES ABOUT THE AUTHOR
JOHN STEINBECK

STEINBECK, John (1902-68). Winner of the 1962 Nobel prize for literature, the American author John Steinbeck is best remembered for his novel 'The Grapes of Wrath'. Steinbeck's story of a family of farm workers migrating from Oklahoma to California describes the hopelessness of the Great Depression era.

John Ernst Steinbeck was born on Feb. 27, 1902, in Salinas, Calif. He took classes at Stanford University for several years but left without a degree. He worked as a laborer to support himself while he wrote. Steinbeck's first novel was published in 1929, but it was not until the publication of 'Tortilla Flat' in 1935 that he attained critical and popular acclaim.

He followed this success with 'In Dubious Battle' (1936) and 'Of Mice and Men' (1937). 'The Grapes of Wrath' (1939) earned for Steinbeck a Pulitzer prize. In these works Steinbeck's proletarian themes are expressed through his portrayal of the inarticulate, dispossessed laborers who populate his American landscape. Both 'Of Mice and Men' and 'The Grapes of Wrath' were made into motion pictures.

In 1943 Steinbeck traveled to North Africa and Italy as a war correspondent. Some of his later works include 'Cannery Row' (1945), 'The Pearl' (1947), 'East of Eden' (1952), 'The Winter of Our Discontent' (1961), and 'Travels with Charley' (1962). He also wrote several motion-picture scripts, including adaptations of two of his shorter works-'The Pearl' and 'The Red Pony'. Steinbeck died in New York City on Dec. 20, 1968.

---- Courtesy of Compton's Learning Company

INTRODUCTION

This unit has been designed to develop students' reading, writing, thinking, and language skills through exercises and activities related to *Of Mice and Men* by John Steinbeck. It includes fifteen lessons, supported by extra resource materials.

The **introductory lesson** introduces students to one main theme of the novel (friendship) through a bulletin board activity. Following the introductory activity, students are given an explanation of how the activity relates to the book they are about to read.

The **reading assignments** are approximately thirty pages each; some are a little shorter while others are a little longer. Students have approximately 15 minutes of pre-reading work to do prior to each reading assignment. This pre-reading work involves reviewing the study questions for the assignment and doing some vocabulary work for 8 to 10 vocabulary words they will encounter in their reading.

The **study guide questions** are fact-based questions; students can find the answers to these questions right in the text. These questions come in two formats: short answer or multiple choice The best use of these materials is probably to use the short answer version of the questions as study guides for students (since answers will be more complete), and to use the multiple choice version for occasional quizzes. If your school has the appropriate machinery, it might be a good idea to make transparencies of your answer keys for the overhead projector.

The **vocabulary work** is intended to enrich students' vocabularies as well as to aid in the students' understanding of the book. Prior to each reading assignment, students will complete a two-part worksheet for approximately 8 to 10 vocabulary words in the upcoming reading assignment. Part I focuses on students' use of general knowledge and contextual clues by giving the sentence in which the word appears in the text. Students are then to write down what they think the words mean based on the words' usage. Part II nails down the definitions of the words by giving students dictionary definitions of the words and having students match the words to the correct definitions based on the words' contextual usage. Students should then have a thorough understanding of the words when they meet them in the text.

After each reading assignment, students will go back and formulate answers for the study guide questions. Discussion of these questions serves as a **review** of the most important events and ideas presented in the reading assignments.

After students complete extra discussion questions, there is a **vocabulary review** lesson which pulls together all of the fragmented vocabulary lists for the reading assignments and gives students a review of all of the words they have studied.

Following the reading of the book, two lessons are devoted to the **extra discussion questions/writing assignments**. These questions focus on interpretation, critical analysis and personal response, employing a variety of thinking skills and adding to the students' understanding of the novel. These questions are done as a **group activity**. Using the information they have acquired so far through individual work and class discussions, students get together to further examine the text and to brainstorm ideas relating to the themes of the novel.

The group activity is followed by a **reports and discussion** session in which the groups share their ideas about the book with the entire class; thus, the entire class gets exposed to many different ideas regarding the themes and events of the book.

There are three **writing assignments** in this unit, each with the purpose of informing, persuading, or having students express personal opinions. The first assignment is to inform: students compose a "want ad" in which they advertise to find a friend. This assignment pulls in the theme of friendship and the skills necessary to write a "want ad." The second assignment gives students the opportunity to express their personal ideas: students choose a hope or dream that they have for the future and make a plan they can follow to help make their dreams come true. The third assignment is to give students a chance to persuade: students pretend to be defending or prosecuting George for Lennie's murder and write their closing arguments to a jury.

In addition, there is a **nonfiction reading assignment**. Students are required to read a piece of nonfiction related in some way to *Of Mice and Men*. After reading their nonfiction pieces, students will fill out a worksheet on which they answer questions regarding facts, interpretation, criticism, and personal opinions. During one class period, students make **oral presentations** about the nonfiction pieces they have read. This not only exposes all students to a wealth of information, it also gives students the opportunity to practice **public speaking**.

There is an optional **class project** (Project Homeless) through which students gain first-hand knowledge of the situation of the homeless people and have some part in helping to do something about this problem.

The **review lesson** pulls together all of the aspects of the unit. The teacher is given four or five choices of activities or games to use which all serve the same basic function of reviewing all of the information presented in the unit.

The **unit test** comes in two formats: all multiple choice-matching-true/false or with a mixture of matching, short answer, and composition. As a convenience, two different tests for each format have been included.

There are additional **support materials** included with this unit. The **extra activities packet** includes suggestions for an in-class library, crossword and word search puzzles related to the novel, and extra vocabulary worksheets. There is a list of **bulletin board ideas** which gives the teacher suggestions for bulletin boards to go along with this unit. In addition, there is a list of **extra class activities** the teacher could choose from to enhance the unit or as a substitution for an exercise the teacher might feel is inappropriate for his/her class. **Answer keys** are located directly after the **reproducible student materials** throughout the unit. The student materials may be reproduced for use in the teacher's classroom without infringement of copyrights. No other portion of this unit may be reproduced without the written consent of Teacher's Pet Publications, Inc.

UNIT OBJECTIVES - *Of Mice and Men*

1. Through reading Steinbeck's *Of Mice and Men*, students will gain a better understanding of the theme of comradeship and the importance of an individual's dreams.

2. Students will demonstrate their understanding of the text on four levels: factual, interpretive, critical and personal.

3. Students will define their own viewpoints on the aforementioned themes.

4. Students will be exposed to a different era of American life, showing many of today's conflicts are not new; they are rooted in our American past.

5. Students will create a plan for achieving at least one of their hopes or dreams.

6. Students will be given the opportunity to practice reading aloud and silently to improve their skills in each area.

7. Students will answer questions to demonstrate their knowledge and understanding of the main events and characters in *Of Mice and Men* as they relate to the author's theme development.

8. Students will enrich their vocabularies and improve their understanding of the novel through the vocabulary lessons prepared for use in conjunction with the novel.

9. The writing assignments in this unit are geared to several purposes:
    a. To have students demonstrate their abilities to inform, to persuade, or to express their own personal ideas
       Note: Students will demonstrate ability to write effectively to <u>inform</u> by developing and organizing facts to convey information. Students will demonstrate the ability to write effectively to <u>persuade</u> by selecting and organizing relevant information, establishing an argumentative purpose, and by designing an appropriate strategy for an identified audience. Students will demonstrate the ability to write effectively to <u>express personal ideas</u> by selecting a form and its appropriate elements.
    b. To check the students' reading comprehension
    c. To make students think about the ideas presented by the novel
    d. To encourage logical thinking
    e. To provide an opportunity to practice good grammar and improve students' use of the English language.

READING ASSIGNMENT SHEET - *Of Mice and Men*

Date Assigned	Reading Assignment (Chapters)	Completion Date
	1	
	2	
	3	
	4	
	5	
	6	

UNIT OUTLINE - *Of Mice and Men*

1 Introduction Writing Assignment 1	2 Materials PVR Ch. 1	3 Study ?s Ch. 1 PVR Ch. 2	4 Writing Assignment 2 PV Ch. 3	5 Study ?s Ch. 2 Read Ch. 3 PVR Ch. 4
6 Study ?s Chs. 3-4 PVR Chs. 5-6	7 Study ?s Chs. 5-6 Writing Conf. Grammar Wksht	8 Grammar Review Working Session	9 Extra Discussion Questions	10 Extra Discussion Questions
11 Vocabulary Review	12 Writing Assignment 3	13 Nonfiction Discussion	14 Review	15 Test
16 Project Homeless	17	18	19	20

Key: P = Preview Study Questions   V = Vocabulary Work   R = Read

STUDY GUIDE QUESTIONS

SHORT ANSWER STUDY GUIDE QUESTIONS - *Of Mice and Men*

Chapter 1
1. Identify and give a physical description of Lennie and George.
2. What is George's first complaint to Lennie?
3. What trouble did George and Lennie have in Weed?
4. What is in Lennie's pocket? Why does he have it?
5. George bursts into a long speech about what he could do if he were alone. What could he do?
6. Lennie offers to go away and live in a cave. What is George's response?
7. Why are George and Lennie different from the other "guys like us that work on ranches"?
8. What are George and Lennie going to do someday?
9. What two things does George want Lennie to remember?
10. Why did George want to camp overnight instead of going another quarter of a mile to the ranch?

Chapter 2
1. What does George answer when the boss asks what he is trying to put over?
2. Identify and describe Curley.
3. The swamper said, "Seems like Curley ain't givin' nobody a chance." Explain.
4. What advice does George give Lennie after Curley and the swamper leave?
5. Identify Slim and Carlson.
6. What does Slim have that Lennie wants?

Chapter 3
1. Slim and George have a long conversation. Slim says it's funny how George and Lennie go around together. What is George's answer?
2. Identify Candy.
3. What did Carlson do with his Luger? Why?
4. What card game does George play?
5. Describe Curley's wife. What's the problem about her?
6. What will Lennie's job be when he and George get their land?
7. What does Candy want when he hears about George's and Lennie's plans? What is he willing to contribute?
8. Why did Curley fight with Lennie? What happened?

Mice and Men Short Answer Study Questions Page 2

Chapter 4
1. Identify Crooks.
2. Lennie tells Crooks about the land. What is his reply at first?
3. What does Crooks want when he believes there might really be land?
4. Why did Curley's wife come to the barn?
5. Why did Crooks change his mind after Curley's wife left?

Chapter 5
1. What happened to Lennie's puppy? What is his reaction?
2. Why did Curley's wife come to see Lennie?
3. What did she tell Lennie?
4. Why did Lennie kill Curley's wife?
5. What was George's reaction when he found out about Curley's wife's death?
6. What was Curley's reaction to his wife's death?

Chapter 6
1. How and why did George kill Lennie?
2. Who is the only one who really understands what George did?
3. Would George ever get a piece of land?

ANSWER KEY: SHORT ANSWER STUDY GUIDE QUESTIONS - *Of Mice and Men*

Chapter 1

1. Identify and give a physical description of Lennie and George.

    Lennie was a huge man, shapeless of face with large, pale eyes, with wide, sloping shoulders, and he walked heavily, dragging his feet a little. Lennie is George's friend, who is not very smart but is an extremely strong man and a good worker.

    George was small and quick, dark of face, with restless eyes and sharp, strong features. He had small, strong hands, slender arms, a thin and bony nose. George took care of Lennie as they traveled together.

2. What is George's first complaint to Lennie?

    George's first complaint is that Lennie is drinking too much water. This is just the first of a series of complaints George has about Lennie. He is almost always complaining about Lennie, but that doesn't change the fact that he appreciates Lennie's companionship.

3. What trouble did George and Lennie have in Weed?

    All we learn in chapter 1 is that some men came after George and Lennie for something they had done. We later learn that apparently Lennie touched a girl's dress to feel the material. When she tried to move, he got excited and confused and held on even tighter. The girl accused him of trying to rape her, and that's when the men came looking for him.

4. What is in Lennie's pocket? Why does he have it?

    A dead mouse is in Lennie's pocket. He has it because he likes to pet soft things.

5. George bursts into a long speech about what he could do if he were alone. What could he do?

    He could take his money and go to a cat house or out drinking whiskey all night or spend his time playing cards at a pool hall; in short, the things the lonely ranch hands do.

6. Lennie offers to go away and live in a cave. What is George's response?

    He tells Lennie that Lennie wouldn't survive, that he couldn't find any food or take care of himself. Then, he admits to Lennie that he doesn't want him to go.

7. Why are George and Lennie different from the other "guys like us that work on ranches"?

    They are different because each one has the other to look out for him.

8. What are George and Lennie going to do someday?

    Someday George and Lennie are going to have a little piece of land with a little shack. They'll have some animals and some crops -- especially a little alfalfa patch so Lennie can pick it and feed the rabbits. They're going to live off the fat of the land, where no one can tell them to get out or boss them around.

9. What two things does George want Lennie to remember?

   George wants Lennie to remember to not say anything when they talk to the boss and to return to this campsite if he gets into trouble.

10. Why did George want to camp overnight instead of going another quarter of a mile to the ranch?

    At the ranch in the evening there would be too many people for Lennie to deal with at once; he might get confused. Also, it would give Lennie a chance to prove himself as a good worker before everyone would discover how slow he was mentally.

Chapter 2

1. What does George answer when the boss asks what he is trying to put over?

   He says he isn't trying to put anything over, that he and Lennie travel together; they are cousins. He says that Lennie is slow mentally because he got kicked in the head by a horse, but that he is a strong, good worker who follows orders well.

2. Identify and describe Curley.

   Curley was the boss' son. He was a young man with a brown face, brown eyes and a head of tightly curled hair. He wore a work glove on his left hand, and he wore high-heeled boots. Curley was a little man, but had been a boxing champion. He didn't like anybody and was always picking fights.

3. The swamper said, "Seems like Curley ain't givin' nobody a chance." Explain.

   If Curley would fight a big man and win, everyone would think he was very strong and would congratulate him. If Curley would fight a big man and lose, everyone would feel sorry for him and tell the big man to pick on someone his own size. Either way, Curley would come out the favorite of the crowd.

4. What advice does George give Lennie after Curley and the swamper leave?

   George tells Lennie to stay away from Curley, that he is nothing but trouble. Lennie replies that he doesn't like this place, and he wants to leave.

5. Identify Slim and Carlson.

   Slim and Carlson are other ranch hands. Slim seems very reasonable and respected and tries to understand George and Lennie. Carlson is later responsible for killing Candy's dog.

6. What does Slim have that Lennie wants?

   Slim's dog has just had a litter of puppies. Lennie wants one.

Chapter 3

1. Slim and George have a long conversation. Slim says it's funny how George and Lennie go around together. What is George's answer?

    He explains that Lennie had no one else to take care of him, and George assumed the responsibility. He admits that Lennie is a pain in the neck sometimes, but that "you kinda get used to going around with a guy and after a while you can't get rid of 'm."

2. Identify Candy.

    Candy is the swamper. He is an older man who has at some time lost one hand. He has an old dog he raised from a pup and although he realizes that the dog must be in misery, he can't bring himself to shoot it.

3. What did Carlson do with his Luger? Why?

    Carlson shot Candy's dog to put it out of its misery because Candy couldn't bring himself to do it.

4. What card game does George play?

    George plays solitaire.

5. Describe Curley's wife. What's the problem about her?

    Curley's wife dresses and acts like a tramp, according to the men. The problem is that she is lonesome since Curley won't let her talk to anyone. She keeps coming around the bunkhouse and barn to talk to the men (and to make advances), and then Curley gets jealous and mad with the men and tries to start fights.

6. What will Lennie's job be when he and George get their land?

    Lennie's job will be to tend the rabbits.

7. What does Candy want when he hears about George's and Lennie's plans? What is he willing to contribute?

    Candy wants to join George and Lennie on their land. He is willing to put up several hundred dollars he has saved.

8. Why did Curley fight with Lennie? What happened?

    Lennie was smiling, thinking about the land when Carlson and Candy were verbally attacking Curley. Curley sees Lennie smiling and assumes he is laughing at him. Curley begins beating on Lennie, who remains with his hands at his sides until George tells him several times to go ahead and fight back. Lennie grabs Curley's hand, and although he wasn't trying to hurt him, he crushes the hand, breaking several bones.

Chapter 4

1. Identify Crooks.

    Crooks is the black stable hand. He has apparently worked on this ranch for some time, judging from his accumulated possessions.

2. Lennie tells Crooks about the land. What is his reply at first?

    Crooks tells Lennie that he is nuts. He says he's seen hundreds of hands come and go with the same dream of having a piece of land, and none of them ever actually did get any land. "Nobody gets to heaven, and nobody gets no land. It's just in their head."

3. What does Crooks want when he believes there might really be land?

    He wants to join the men on the land and will work for free, for just being able to live there.

4. Why did Curley's wife come to the barn?

    She was looking for Curley, she said, but she actually came to talk to the men and find some company.

5. Why did Crooks change his mind after Curley's wife left?

    He realized that the dream could never come true for him. He was a Negro who had just been put in his place by a white woman, and this fact brought back the harsh reality of his life.

Chapter 5

1. What happened to Lennie's puppy? What is his reaction?

    Lennie's puppy died because he handled it too roughly. He knows George is going to be mad, and he thinks George won't let him tend the rabbits now.

2. Why did Curley's wife come to see Lennie?

    Curley's wife came to see Lennie because she figured out that he crushed Curley's hand and wouldn't be afraid of Curley anymore -- he was the most likely candidate for her advances at this time.

3. What did she tell Lennie?

    She told Lennie that she didn't like Curley and that she had had other opportunities to go places and make something of herself, but she couldn't take advantage of them, so she married Curley as the next most likely way to get out of her hometown.

4. Why did Lennie kill Curley's wife?

    Curley's wife invited him to feel her soft hair. As we may have guessed from the foreshadowing event in Weed, he gets a little too rough and when Curley's wife starts to struggle, he gets confused and holds even tighter. When she starts to yell, Lennie thinks George will hear and will be mad that he is communicating with the woman, so he covers her mouth. Lennie gets more and more confused as to what to do (thinking that between the puppy's death and his talking to Curley's wife, George is going to be furious). Finally, he shakes her and her neck snaps.

5. What was George's reaction when he found out about Curley's wife's death?
   He didn't want the men to think he had anything to do with it, and then he tried to think how he could protect Lennie. He went and got his hat and coat and the Luger before he joined the men.

6. What was Curley's reaction to his wife's death?
   Curley was furious, and right away assumed Lennie had done it. He was out for revenge to kill Lennie.

<u>Chapter 6</u>
1. How and why did George kill Lennie?
   George met Lennie at the old campsite and tried to tell him he wasn't mad. He realized that the only way to protect Lennie from the devastating punishment which would be inflicted upon him was to kill him. He made up with Lennie and talked to him about the land, making Lennie look across the water to "see" it. Then he shot him with the Luger in the most humane way possible. George did what he had to do as Lennie's friend.

2. Who is the only one who really understands what George did?
   When the men arrived, Slim was the only one who could sympathize with George. Because of their earlier conversation, he understood the relationship between George and Lennie.

3. Would George ever get a piece of land?
   No, he realized that it was just a dream that would never come true.

MULTIPLE CHOICE FORMAT STUDY GUIDE/QUIZ QUESTIONS - *Of Mice and Men*

Chapter 1

1. Lennie was
    a. a huge man, very strong, not very smart.
    b. small and quick.
    c. short and squat.
    d. fat and lazy.

2. George was
    a. a huge man, very strong, not very smart.
    b. small and quick.
    c. short and squat.
    d. fat and lazy.

3. What was George's first complaint to Lennie?
    a. that Lennie ate too much
    b. that Lennie was lazy
    c. that Lennie drank too much water
    d. that Lennie couldn't read

4. What trouble did George and Lennie have in Weed?
    a. They got drunk and rowdy.
    b. They got fired.
    c. They lost all their money playing cards.
    d. They did something & men came after them.

5. What was in Lennie's pocket?
    a. a dead mouse
    b. a can of beans
    c. a gun
    d. a rabbit

6. What does George say he could do if he were alone?
    a. go to a "cat house"
    b. drink whiskey all night
    c. play cards at a pool hall all night
    d. all of the above

Mice and Men Study/Quiz Questions Multiple Choice Format Page 2

7. Lennie offers to go away and live in a cave. What is George's response?
    a. He punches Lennie.
    b. He tells Lennie that he doesn't want him to go.
    c. He helps him pack his gear.
    d. none of the above

8. Why are George and Lennie different from the other "guys like [them] that work on ranches"?
    a. Each has the other to look out for him.
    b. They are not drifters.
    c. They like their work and want to do it forever.
    d. They are actually wealthy.

9. What are George and Lennie going to do someday?
    a. have a little piece of land
    b. have some animals and crops
    c. live off the fat of the land
    d. all of the above

10. What things does George want Lennie to remember?
    a. not to say anything to the boss
    b. to tell the boss what a good worker he is
    c. to return to the campsite if he gets into trouble
    d. A & C

11. Why did George want to camp overnight instead of going another quarter of a mile to the ranch?
    a. He was too tired.
    b. He was looking out for Lennie's best interests.
    c. He didn't like crowds.
    d. He didn't want to work any sooner than he had to.

Mice and Men Study/Quiz Questions Multiple Choice Format Page 3

Chapter 2

1. What does George answer when the boss asks what he is trying to put over?
    a. He explains that he looks out for Lennie, who got kicked in the head and is slow.
    b. He explains that Lennie can't talk for himself.
    c. He doesn't say anything; he just looks at the ground.
    d. He gives the boss a dirty look and says, "Nothin'."

2. Curley was
    a. the boss's son.
    b. a boxing champion.
    c. a little man.
    d. all of the above

3. The swamper said, "Seems like Curley ain't givin' nobody a chance." What did he mean?
    a. If Curley fought the big man and won, everyone would congratulate him.
    b. If Curley fought the big man and lost, everyone would feel sorry for him.
    c. Curley would come out the favorite of the crowd.
    d. All of the above.

4. What advice does George give Lennie after Curley and the swamper leave?
    a. keep the mouse in his pocket
    b. stay away from Curley
    c. be very quiet
    d. go to bed

5. Who is a ranch hand who is reasonable and respected and tries to understand George and Lennie?
    a. Carlson
    b. Swamper
    c. Slim
    d. Curley

6. What does Slim have that Lennie wants?
    a. puppies
    b. a gun
    c. a wife
    d. the best bunk

Mice and Men Study/Quiz Questions Multiple Choice Format Page 4

<u>Chapter 3</u>
1. What does Slim think is funny about George and Lennie?
    a. that they have no past
    b. that they go around together
    c. that they have no families
    d. A & C

2. Who is the swamper?
    a. Slim
    b. Carlson
    c. Lennie
    d. Candy

3. What did Carlson do with his Luger?
    a. shot Lennie
    b. shot Candy's dog
    c. hid it
    d. gave it to Slim

4. What card game does George play?
    a. poker
    b. bridge
    c. solitaire
    d. rummy

5. Curley's wife
    a. dresses and acts like a tramp.
    b. is lonesome.
    c. makes advances to the ranch hands.
    d. all of the above

6. What will Lennie's job be when he and George get their land?
    a. tend the rabbits
    b. milk the cow
    c. plow the fields
    d. cook

Mice and Men Study/Quiz Questions Multiple Choice Format Page 5

7. What does Candy want when he hears about George's and Lennie's plans?
    a. He wants George and Lennie to go away and stop talking about such foolishness.
    b. He wants them to give him money.
    c. He wants to join them.
    d. B & C

8. Why did Curley fight with Lennie?
    a. Lennie punched him first.
    b. They both wanted the same puppy.
    c. Curley thought Lennie was laughing at him.
    d. Lennie made a rude remark about Curley's wife.

Mice and Men Study/Quiz Questions Multiple Choice Format Page 6

<u>Chapter 4</u>
1. Crooks is
 a. the cook.
 b. the swamper.
 c. the stable hand.
 d. a range rider.

2. Lennie tells Crooks about the land. What is his first reply?
 a. "Nobody gets to heaven, and nobody gets no land."
 b. Crooks wants in on the deal, too.
 c. "Quit talking foolishness and get back to work."
 d. Crooks sneers and walks away.

3. What does Crooks want when he believes there might really be land?
 a. He wants George's money.
 b. He want's Lennie's deed and is willing to do anything to get it.
 c. He wants George to help him find some land of his own, too.
 d. He wants to join Lennie and George.

4. Why did Curley's wife come to the barn?
 a. She wanted to be alone.
 b. She wanted some company.
 c. She wanted to make Lennie mad.
 d. She was looking for a puppy.

5. Why did Crooks change his mind after Curley's wife left?
 a. She reminded Crooks of the harsh realities of his own life.
 b. He didn't like the way George and Lennie treated Curley's wife, and decided he didn't want to be associated with them.
 c. He was afraid.
 d. He had to give her all his money.

Mice and Men Study/Quiz Questions Multiple Choice Format Page 7

Chapter 5

1. What happened to Lennie's puppy?
    a. George killed it.
    b. Carlson killed it.
    c. Lennie killed it.
    d. It ran away.

2. Why did Curley's wife come to see Lennie?
    a. She wanted to give him a new puppy.
    b. She had fallen in love with him since he was so shy and loveable.
    c. She figured Lennie wouldn't be afraid of Curley & Curley would be afraid of Lennie.
    d. She wanted to hear about the land he and George were going to buy.

3. What did Curley's wife tell Lennie?
    a. She had married Curley just to get out of her hometown.
    b. She didn't like Curley.
    c. She had had opportunities but couldn't take advantage of them.
    d. all of the above

4. Why did Lennie kill Curley's wife?
    a. He was confused and just wanted her to keep quiet and still; it was an accident.
    b. He didn't mean to; she made him angry, and he had hit her too hard before he realized what he was doing.
    c. He didn't like being teased.
    d. She wouldn't believe that he and George were going to have land and rabbits someday, so he shook her and snapped her neck by mistake.

5. What was George's reaction when he found out about Curley's wife's death?
    a. He was furious.
    b. He tried to figure out how to best protect Lennie.
    c. He was totally shocked.
    d. He immediately ran after Lennie to yell at him.

6. What was Curley's reaction to his wife's death?
    a. He was glad to be rid of her.
    b. He didn't care one way or the other.
    c. He was furious and wanted revenge.
    d. He was sad, but realized it was an accident.

Mice and Men Study/Quiz Questions Multiple Choice Format Page 8

<u>Chapter 6</u>
1. Who killed Lennie?
	a. Curley
	b. Candy
	c. Slim
	d. George

2. Who was the only one who understood what George did?
	a. Curley
	b. Candy
	c. Slim
	d. Crooks

3. Would George ever get a piece of land?
	a. Yes, he and Candy were making plans together.
	b. Yes, he wanted to get the land for Lennie's sake.
	c. No, he realized that it was just a dream that would never come true.
	d. No, he never really wanted it anyway.

ANSWER KEY - MULTIPLE CHOICE STUDY/QUIZ QUESTIONS
Of Mice and Men

Chapter 1	Chapter 2	Chapter 3	Chapter 4
1. A	1. A	1. B	1. C
2. B	2. D	2. D	2. A
3. C	3. D	3. B	3. D
4. D	4. B	4. C	4. B
5. A	5. C	5. D	5. A
6. D	6. A	6. A	
7. B		7. C	
8. A		8. C	
9. D			
10. D			
11. B			

Chapter 5	Chapter 6
1. C	1. D
2. C	2. C
3. D	3. C
4. A	
5. B	
6. C	

PREREADING VOCABULARY WORKSHEETS

VOCABULARY - *Of Mice and Men*

Chapter 1 Part I: Using Prior Knowledge and Contextual Clues

Below are the sentences in which the vocabulary words appear in the text. Read the sentence. Use any clues you can find in the sentence combined with your prior knowledge, and write what you think the underlined words mean in the space provided.

1. George stared morosely at the water.

2. But Lennie made an elaborate pantomime of innocence.

3. Lennie hesitated, backed away, looked wildly at the brush line as though he contemplated running for his freedom.

4. Lennie reluctantly reached into his pocket.

5. Lennie sat down on the ground and hung his head dejectedly.

6. He took on the elaborate manner of little girls when they are mimicking one another.

7. He looked across the fire at Lennie's anguished face, and then he looked ashamedly at the flames.

8. George gestured with his spoon.

Vocabulary - *Of Mice and Men* Chapter 1 Continued

Part II: Determining the Meaning
   Match the vocabulary words to their dictionary definitions.

___ 1. morosely   A. showing a feeling of guilt
___ 2. pantomime   B. imitating
___ 3. contemplated   C. unwillingly; hesitantly
___ 4. reluctantly   D. acting that consists mostly of gestures; no words
___ 5. dejectedly   E. made a motion to express thought or emphasize speech
___ 6. mimicking   F. showing an agonizing physical or mental pain
___ 7. anguished   G. considered thoughtfully
___ 8. ashamedly   H. sadly; depressed or disheartened
___ 9. gestured   I. glumly; gloomily

Vocabulary - *Of Mice and Men* Chapter 2

Part I: Using Prior Knowledge and Contextual Clues
　　Below are the sentences in which the vocabulary words appear in the text. Read the sentence. Use any clues you can find in the sentence combined with your prior knowledge, and write what you think the underlined words mean in the space provided.

1. "I ain't so sure," said George skeptically.

2. "Damn right he don't," said George, slightly mollified, "not if he wants to stay workin' long."

3. He said ominously, "Well, he better watch out for Lennie."

4. He had drawn a derogatory statement from George.

5. "I don't want no trouble," he said plaintively.

6. His face contorted with thought.

7. She was suddenly apprehensive.

8. There was a gravity in his manner and a quiet so profound that all talk stopped when he spoke.

9. Lennie, who had been following the conversation back and forth with his eyes, smiled complacently at the compliment.

10. Carlson stepped back to let Slim precede him, and then the two of them went out the door.

Vocabulary - *Of Mice and Men* Chapter 2 Continued

Part II: Determining the Meaning -- Match the vocabulary words to their dictionary definitions.

___ 10. skeptically   A. uneasy; anxious
___ 11. mollified   B. in a self-satisfied manner
___ 12. ominously   C. showing doubt or disbelief; questioningly
___ 13. derogatory   D. twisted or strained out of shape
___ 14. plaintively   E. pacified; calmed
___ 15. contorted   F. complete; coming from the depth of one's being
___ 16. apprehensive   G. detracting or disparaging
___ 17. profound   H. mournfully; sorrowfully
___ 18. complacently   I. go before
___ 19. precede   J. with foreboding

Vocabulary - *Of Mice and Men* Chapter 3

Part I: Using Prior Knowledge and Contextual Clues
   Below are the sentences in which the vocabulary words appear in the text. Read the sentence. Use any clues you can find in the sentence combined with your prior knowledge, and write what you think the underlined words mean in the space provided.

1. He reached down and picked the tiny puppy from where Lennie had been concealing it against his stomach.

2. Slim gazed at him for a moment and then looked down at his hands; he subdued one hand with the other, and held it down.

3. Whit laid down his cards impressively.

4. He subsided, grumbling to himself, threatening the future cats which might dare to disturb future rabbits.

5. George sat entranced with his own picture.

6. When Candy spoke they both jumped as though they had been caught doing something reprehensible.

7. They all sat still, all bemused by the beauty of the thing, each mind was popped into the future when this lovely thing should come about.

Part II: Determining the Meaning   Match the vocabulary words to their dictionary definitions.

___ 20. concealing   A. fascinated
___ 21. subdued   B. put into deep thought
___ 22. impressively   C. settled down
___ 23. subsided   D. to quiet or bring under control by physical force
___ 24. entranced   E. worthy of blame; deserving censure
___ 25. reprehensible   F. hiding
___ 26. bemused   G. commanding attention; making a strong impression

Vocabulary - *Of Mice and Men* Chapter 4

Part I: Using Prior Knowledge and Contextual Clues

Below are the sentences in which the vocabulary words appear in the text. Read the sentence. Use any clues you can find in the sentence combined with your prior knowledge, and write what you think the underlined words mean in the space provided.

1. And he had books, too; a tattered dictionary and a <u>mauled</u> copy of the California civil code for 1905.

2. In the stable buck's room a small electric globe threw a <u>meager</u> yellow light.

3. Crooks scowled, but Lennie's <u>disarming</u> smile defeated him.

4. His voice grew soft and <u>persuasive</u>.

5. She paused and her face lost its <u>sullenness</u> and grew interested.

6. "Awright," she said <u>contemptuously</u>.

7. She was breathless with <u>indignation</u>.

8. She <u>appraised</u> him coolly.

Vocabulary - *Of Mice and Men* Chapter 4 Continued

Part II: Determining the Meaning
Match the vocabulary words to their dictionary definitions.

___ 27. mauled
___ 28. meager
___ 29. disarming
___ 30. persuasive
___ 31. sullenness
___ 32. contemptuously
___ 33. indignation
___ 34. appraised

A. gloominess
B. handled roughly; beaten up
C. an anger aroused by something unjust, mean or unworthy
D. evaluated
E. convincing
F. deficient in quantity; scant
G. endearing, tending to remove hostility or suspicion
H. with a feeling of contempt; scornfully

Vocabulary - *Of Mice and Men* Chapter 5

Part I: Using Prior Knowledge and Contextual Clues
   Below are the sentences in which the vocabulary words appear in the text. Read the sentence. Use any clues you can find in the sentence combined with your prior knowledge, and write what you think the underlined words mean in the space provided.

1. She consoled him. "Don't you worry none. He was jus' a mutt. You can get another one easy."

2. And because she had confided in him, she moved closer to Lennie and sat beside him.

3. Her feet battered on the hay and she writhed to be free; and from under Lennie's hand came a muffled screaming.

4. For a moment he seemed bewildered.

5. "Then--it's all off?" Candy said sulkily.

6. He sniveled, and his voice shook.

Part II: Determining the Meaning
   Match the vocabulary words to their dictionary definitions. If there are words for which you cannot figure out the definition by contextual clues and by process of elimination, look them up in a dictionary.

___ 35. consoled
___ 36. confided
___ 37. writhed
___ 38. bewildered
___ 39. sulkily
___ 40. sniveled

A. twisted
B. comforted
C. confused; befuddled
D. gloomily
E. told private matters not intended for public knowledge
F. cried or wept with sniffling

Vocabulary - *Of Mice and Men* Chapter 6

Part I: Using Prior Knowledge and Contextual Clues
　　Below are the sentences in which the vocabulary words appear in the text. Read the sentence. Use any clues you can find in the sentence combined with your prior knowledge, and write what you think the underlined words mean.

1. Now Lennie <u>retorted</u> <u>belligerently</u>, "He ain't neither."

2. His voice was <u>monotonous</u>, had no emphasis.

3. Lennie jarred, and then settled slowly forward to the sand, and he lay without <u>quivering</u>.

Part II: Determining the Meaning
　　Match the vocabulary words to their dictionary definitions. If there are words for which you cannot figure out the definition by contextual clues and by process of elimination, look them up in a dictionary.

___ 41. retorted　　　　　　A. trembling
___ 42. belligerently　　　　B. replied sharply
___ 43. monotonous　　　　C. hostilely; aggressively
___ 44. quivering　　　　　D. unvarying the vocal tone or pitch

ANSWER KEY - VOCABULARY
Of Mice and Men

Chapter 1	Chapter 2	Chapter 3	Chapter 4	Chapter 5	Chapter 6
1. I	10. C	20. F	27. B	35. B	41. B
2. D	11. E	21. D	28. F	36. E	42. C
3. G	12. J	22. G	29. G	37. A	43. D
4. C	13. G	23. C	30. E	38. C	44. A
5. H	14. H	24. A	31. A	39. D	
6. B	15. D	25. E	32. H	40. F	
7. F	16. A	26. B	33. C		
8. A	17. F		34. D		
9. E	18. B				
	19. I				

DAILY LESSONS

LESSON ONE

Objectives
    1. To introduce the *Of Mice and Men* unit
    2. To distribute books and other related materials
    3. To introduce the theme of "people need friends"
    4. To give students the opportunity to write to inform by developing and organizing facts to convey information

NOTE: Prior to Lesson One you need to have assigned for students to bring to class pictures showing things that friends do for each other. Also, you should have an empty bulletin board with just background paper and the title: OF MICE AND MEN; A STORY ABOUT FRIENDSHIP.

Activity #1

    Tell students to get out the pictures they were assigned to bring to class. Have each student post his picture(s) on the bulletin board and, as he does so, to explain to the class what trait of friendship his picture exemplifies.

TRANSITION: Explain to students that *Of Mice and Men*, the book they are about to read, is a story about friendship--about what it really means to be someone's friend and to have a friend.

Activity #2

    Distribute Writing Assignment #1 and discuss the directions in detail. Give students the remainder of this class period to work on this assignment. While students are working on this assignment, distribute/assign the books to students. (If you wish, you may also distribute the other materials which students will need for the unit. There is, however, time planned for distributing materials in Lesson Two. If your students tend to lose materials or tend to forget to bring what they need to class, you might wait to give the materials out in Lesson Two when you will also need students' attention to tell them how these materials are to be used.)

WRITING ASSIGNMENT #1 - *Of Mice and Men*

PROMPT

Loneliness is a common emotion that everyone feels once in a while--some more often than others. The ranch hands in *Of Mice and Men* were drifters; they had no families close by and didn't stay in one place long enough to make lasting friends. Theirs was a lonely lifestyle. Two fellows, George and Lennie, found friendship early in their lives and traveled together. From them we can see what it means to be a friend and what it means to have a friend. Friendship has great rewards, but being a friend isn't always easy.

Your assignment is to design an advertisement -- "WANTED: A FRIEND". Your advertisement should carry all the usual information in a "want ad": what you want, a job description, the requirements and the rewards. Your ad must fit on an 8 1/2" X 11" sheet of paper. Be as creative as you like, but remember your ad must contain the information requested above and remember that you are striving for an effective advertisement.

PREWRITING

The first thing you need to do is to jot down ideas you have about what a friend's job description would contain. What does it mean to be a friend? What qualities are necessary for a person to have to be a good friend? What are the positive aspects of being a friend? What are the difficult parts of the job?

Put down all of your thoughts, and then go back and sort through them. Combine ideas that are essentially the same. Organize your thoughts into categories: job description, qualifications/requirements, and rewards. From there you can begin to design your ad.

DRAFTING

You need to make a few basic decisions: Are you going to have any graphics (drawings) in your ad? What will be the attention-getter in your ad? How can you make all of your most important information fit on one page? How will you lay-out or design your ad? (How will it look on the page?) Once you have decided these things, you can put pencil to paper and make a rough draft of your ad.

PROMPT

After you have finished a rough draft of your ad, revise it yourself until you are happy with your work. Then, ask a student who sits near you to tell you what he/she likes best about your work, and what things he/she thinks can be improved. Take another look at your ad keeping in mind your critic's suggestions, and make the revisions you feel are necessary.

PROOFREADING

Do a final proofreading of your paper double-checking your grammar, spelling, organization, and the clarity of your ideas.

LESSON TWO

Objectives
1. To distribute and discuss the materials students will use in this unit
2. To discuss PROJECT HOMELESS, a project that goes along with this unit
3. To do the prereading work for chapter 1
4. To read chapter 1
5. To give students practice reading orally
6. To evaluate students' oral reading

Activity #1
Distribute the materials students will use in this unit. Explain in detail how students are to use these materials.

Study Guides Students should preview the study guide questions before each reading assignment to get a feeling for what events and ideas are important in that section. After reading the section, students will (as a class or individually) answer the questions to review the important events and ideas from that section of the book. Students should keep the study guides as study materials for the unit test.

Vocabulary   Prior to reading a reading assignment, students will do vocabulary work related to the section of the book they are about to read. Following the completion of the reading of the book, there will be a vocabulary review of all the words used in the vocabulary assignments. Students should keep their vocabulary work as study materials for the unit test.

Reading Assignment Sheet   You need to fill in the reading assignment sheet to let students know when their reading has to be completed. You can either write the assignment sheet on a side blackboard or bulletin board and leave it there for students to see each day, or you can "ditto" copies for each student to have. In either case, you should advise students to become very familiar with the reading assignments so they know what is expected of them.

Extra Activities Center   The Extra Activities Packet portion of this unit contains suggestions for a library of related books and articles in your classroom as well as crossword and word search puzzles. Make an extra activities center in your room where you will keep these materials for students to use. (Bring the books and articles in from the library and keep several copies of the puzzles on hand.) Explain to students that these materials are available for students to use when they finish reading assignments or other class work early.

Nonfiction Assignment Sheet Explain to students that they each are to read at least one non-fiction piece from the in-class library at some time during the unit. Students will fill out a nonfiction assignment sheet after completing the reading to help you evaluate their reading experiences and to help the students think about and evaluate their own reading experiences.

<u>Books</u> Each school has its own rules and regulations regarding student use of school books. Advise students of the procedures that are normal for your school.

Activity #2
If you have decided to do Project Homeless with your students during this unit (instead of after it), take time now to explain what the project is and how the students will do it. (See the information following this lesson for guidelines.)

Activity #3
Have students complete the prereading work for chapter 1 of *Of Mice and Men*. They should review the study questions and do the required vocabulary work.

Activity #4
Have students read chapter 1 of *Of Mice and Men* out loud in class. You probably know the best way to get readers within your class; pick students at random, ask for volunteers, or use whatever method works best for your group. If you have not yet completed an oral reading evaluation for your students this marking period, this would be a good opportunity to do so. A form is included with this unit for your convenience.

If students do not complete reading chapter 1 in class, they should do so prior to your next class meeting.

PROJECT HOMELESS

Objectives:
Project Homeless is a total class project for use in conjunction with the novelette *Of Mice and Men*. Since one of the main themes in the book deals with loneliness and the importance of friendship, what it means to be a good friend, and the lonely life of the men who have no homes of their own, it seems the perfect occasion to make students aware of people in their own cities or towns who are without homes, without food, perhaps without friends and/or are without hope. Someone would have had to have been living under a rock for the last several years to not know that homelessness is a very real problem in the world today. Rather than just giving the homeless more "lip service" this project is intended to make students *see* the problem and to have some part, however small, in *really helping* to do something about the problem.

THE PROJECT
This project is separate from the rest of the *Mice and Men* unit so you can either use it while you are doing the *Mice and Men* unit or as a separate mini-unit after you have completed the unit test for the book. Also, having it as a separate project enables you to eliminate it if you want to or need to for some reason, without disrupting the normal flow of the unit.

Assignment 1 Your local TV station (or perhaps your media center) should have some videotaped reports about the homeless. Find several videotaped reports and show them to your students. Use the video tapes as a springboard for a discussion of the homeless situation.

Assignment 2 Do a group writing assignment for (or have individual students write) a letter of request to your local shelter requesting a person in charge there to come out to your class to discuss the needs of homeless people in your area. Send a letter of request and follow up with a phone call to make the necessary arrangements.

Assignment 3 After students have seen the tapes, send them to the library to do some research. Each student should read and summarize at least two articles about the homeless.

Assignment 4 After students have done their research, have them give oral reports about the articles they have read so that all the students are exposed to the wealth of information that has been collectively read.

Assignment 5 Try to arrange to have a person come from your local shelter to discuss the needs of the homeless in your area. This is the object of Assignment 2. It should be completed prior to Assignment 6 so that students will know what the needs of the homeless are in your area prior to making their plans.

Of Mice and Men Project Homeless page 2

Assignment 6 Divide students into groups of four or five. Explain that their job is to make a list of things that homeless people need and to brainstorm practical ideas about what they personally, as individuals and as a group, can do to help fill those needs. This can get as involved as you, the teacher, want. You may be up for a simple group collection of goods, or you could delve into a whole huge project of fundraisers involving your whole school and your whole community. The more involved you make it, the more your students will learn if they are given the proper guidance and opportunities. See what activities your students suggest.

The planning of these activities, whatever they may turn out to be, should be done in class. Breaking down your class into groups to handle different activities would be a good idea if you are going to run several activities at one time. Each group should be responsible for one activity, and within each group, each person should be given definite responsibilities. You could assign one student to be the group leader, the coordinator for that particular activity.

A certain amount of class time will have to be spent on these plans. It should, however, be a valuable experience for each student because each student will be facing real problems and having to make real decisions concerning real solutions. Organization and scheduling skills will be used; in some cases, letter-writing skills and other communications skills will be necessary. Again, the skills used will depend largely on how involved you make the project and what kinds of projects your students are interested in doing.

Assignment 7 Schedule a visit to your local shelter so students can actually see for what cause their efforts are going. If possible, this assignment should be combined with Assignment 5, having the person from the shelter talk to the students. If it can't be coordinated that way, try at sometime during the project to take your students to the shelter.

Assignment 8 Have students carry out the plans they have made. The types of activities they have planned will determine the amount of class time which will be spent on this project. If most of the work is being done outside of the classroom, be sure to get daily updates from each of your groups and occasionally have a day devoted to Project Homeless work so that students do not lose their enthusiasm or think that just because the work is done out of class, it is unimportant.

Assignment 9 When your Project Homeless activities are complete, take a day to evaluate the success of each project. Discuss the good points of each activity and discuss how things could have been done better. I suggest that you have a writing assignment in which each student evaluates his/her own experiences from the project.

Assignment 10 Have a reception for all the people who were involved with your Project Homeless--anyone who contributed to the success of your project. Let your students plan the reception--it will be another good, real-life skill-builder.

NONFICTION ASSIGNMENT SHEET
(To be completed after reading the required nonfiction article)

Name _____ Date _____

Title of Nonfiction Read _____

Written By _____ Publication Date _____

I. Factual Summary: Write a short summary of the piece you read.

II. Vocabulary
    1. With which vocabulary words in the piece did you encounter some degree of difficulty?

    2. How did you resolve your lack of understanding with these words?

III. Interpretation: What was the main point the author wanted you to get from reading his work?

IV. Criticism
    1. With which points of the piece did you agree or find easy to accept? Why?

    2. With which points of the piece did you disagree or find difficult to believe? Why?

V. Personal Response: What do you think about this piece? <u>OR</u> How does this piece influence your ideas?

ORAL READING EVALUATION - *Of Mice and Men*

Name _____ Class____ Date _____

SKILL	EXCELLENT	GOOD	AVERAGE	FAIR	POOR
Fluency	5	4	3	2	1
Clarity	5	4	3	2	1
Audibility	5	4	3	2	1
Pronunciation	5	4	3	2	1
_____	5	4	3	2	1
_____	5	4	3	2	1

Total _____ Grade _____

Comments:

LESSON THREE

Objectives
1. To review the main events and ideas from chapter 1
2. To preview the study questions for chapter 2
3. To familiarize students with the vocabulary in chapter 2
4. To read chapter 2

Activity #1
Discuss the answers to the study questions for chapter 1 in detail. Write the answers on the board or overhead transparency so students can have the correct answers for study purposes. Note: It is a good practice in public speaking and leadership skills for individual students to take charge of leading the discussions of the study questions. Perhaps a different student could go to the front of the class and lead the discussion each day that the study questions are discussed during this unit. Of course, the teacher should guide the discussion when appropriate and be sure to fill in any gaps the students leave.

Activity #2
Give students about fifteen minutes to preview the study questions for chapter 2 of *Of Mice and Men* and to do the related vocabulary work.

Activity #3
Continue your oral reading evaluations as students read chapter 2 of *Of Mice and Men* orally in class. If students do not complete reading chapter 2 in class, they should do so prior to the next class meeting.

LESSON FOUR

Objectives
    1. To give students the opportunity to practice writing to express personal ideas
    2. To give students the opportunity to practice setting goals and thinking through ways in which they can achieve their goals
    3. To draw attention to the theme of dreams and dreaming in the book
    4. To give the teacher an opportunity to evaluate each student's writing skills
    5. To give students an opportunity to produce an error-free paper and to apply the teacher's suggestions

Activity #1

Distribute Writing Assignment #2 and discuss the directions in detail. Allow the remaining class time for students to complete the assignment. Collect the papers at the end of the class period.

Follow - Up: After you have graded the assignments, have a writing conference with the students. (This unit schedules one in Lesson Eight.) After the writing conference, allow students to revise their papers using your suggestions and corrections. Give them about three days from the date they receive their papers to complete the revision. I suggest grading the revisions on an A-C-E scale (all revisions well-done, some revisions made, few or no revisions made). This will speed your grading time and still give some credit for the students' efforts.

Activity #2

Tell students that prior to the next class period they should have previewed the study questions and done the vocabulary for chapter 3. If they have time after completing the writing assignment, they may begin this assignment in class.

WRITING ASSIGNMENT #2 - *Of Mice and Men*

PROMPT

Everyone has hopes and dreams for the future. We hope our lives will turn out in a certain way; we hope certain events will take place; we hope we will be able to live a certain lifestyle, and so on. George and Lennie dream of having a piece of land, a farm, of their own.

Sometimes we're lucky and things just seem to work out without our doing anything to make them happen. More often, though, we can take certain steps to make our hopes and dreams more likely to come true. That doesn't mean that they will, but the chances of their coming true can be greatly increased.

Your assignment is to choose one of your hopes or dreams for the future, describe it, and make a detailed plan as to what you believe you can do to help make your hope or dream come true.

PREWRITING

A good way to start is to think about your future. What would you like to have happen in the future more than anything else? Jot down what that is on a piece of paper. Make notes about the details of your dream.

Now, stop and think about what you can do to improve your chances of having that dream come true. Make a list of things you can do. Are there some things you should do first, followed by other things? Arrange your list in a logical or chronological order.

DRAFTING

You should begin your paper with an introductory paragraph giving your reader some background describing your hope or dream. Use your notes about the details of your dream to help you get started.

The body of your composition should contain information about the things you can do to help yourself achieve your dream. Take each point that you jotted down and make each one into a topic sentence for a paragraph in the body of your composition. Fill out each paragraph by explaining how this point will help you achieve your goal or by explaining how you can do this thing that will help you achieve your goal.

Write a paragraph in which you conclude how likely it will be that you will actually be able to achieve your goal based on the facts you have presented.

PROOFREADING

When you finish the rough draft of your paper, ask a student who sits near you to read it. After reading your rough draft, he/she should tell you what he/she liked best about your work, which parts were difficult to understand, and ways in which your work could be improved. Reread your paper considering your critic's comments, and make the corrections you think are necessary. Do a final proofreading of your paper double-checking your grammar, spelling, organization, and the clarity of your ideas.

LESSON FIVE

Objectives
    1. To review the main ideas and events of chapter 2
    2. To read chapter 3
    3. To do the prereading vocabulary work for chapter 4
    4. To preview the study questions for chapter 4
    5. To read chapter 4

Activity #1

    Discuss the answers to the study questions for chapter 2 as you did the questions for chapter 1.

Activity #2

    Give students time to read chapter 3 silently in class.

Activity #3

    Tell students that they are to have completed the prereading previewing and vocabulary work for chapter 4 and to have read chapter 4 prior to the next class period. If they have time in class after reading chapter 3, they may begin this assignment.

LESSON SIX

Objectives
    1. To review the main ideas of chapters 3 & 4
    2. To preview the study questions for chapters 5 & 6
    3. To do the prereading vocabulary work for chapters 5 & 6
    4. To read chapters 5 & 6

Activity #1

    Use the multiple choice format of the study questions for chapters 3 & 4 as a quiz to check to make sure students have done the required reading and to review the main ideas of chapters 3 & 4. (If students are using the multiple choice questions, use the short answer format for your quiz.) Give students ample time to answer the questions, and then have students exchange papers for grading. Discuss the answers in detail and make sure students take notes for study purposes.

Activity #2

    Tell students to preview the study questions and do the vocabulary work for chapters 5 & 6.

Activity #3

    Tell students that they should read chapters 5 & 6 prior to your next class meeting. If they have time after completing Activity #2, they may use the remainder of this class period to begin their reading.

LESSON SEVEN

Objectives
    1. To review the main events of chapters 5 & 6
    2. To evaluate students' writing
    3. To have students revise their Writing Assignment 1 papers
    4. To prepare students for a brief grammar review

Activity #1

Discuss the answers to the study questions for chapters 5 & 6 as you have done the study questions previously.

Activity #2

Distribute the Writing/Grammar Review Exercise for *Of Mice and Men*. Discuss the directions in detail. Students should work on this exercise while they are waiting for their writing conferences with you. This worksheet should be completed prior to your next class period.

Activity #3

Call students to your desk (or some other private area) to discuss their papers from Writing Assignment 1. A Writing Evaluation Form is included with this unit to help structure your conferences. Be sure to give students a day and a date for when their revisions are due.

WRITING/GRAMMAR REVIEW EXERCISE
Of Mice and Men

The following passage, taken from *Of Mice and Men*, contains many grammatical errors. Your assignment is to rewrite these paragraphs so that they are perfectly correct in formal, written English.

"What kinda harm am I doin' to you? Seems like they ain't none of them cares how I gotta live. I tell you I ain't used to livin' like this. I coulda made somethin' of myself.... I lived right in Salinas. Come there when I was a kid. Well, a show come through, an' I met one of the actors. He says I could go with that show. But my ol' lady wouldn' let me. She says because I was on'y fifteen. But the guy says I coulda. If I'd went, I wouldn't be livin' like this, you bet....

'Nother time I met a guy, an' he was in pitchers. Went out to the Riverside Dance Palace with him. He says he was gonna put me in the movies. Says I was a natural. Soon's he got back to Hollywood he was gonna write to me about it.... I never got that letter. I always thought my ol' lady stole it. Well, I wasn't gonna stay no place where I couldn't get nowhere or make something of myself, an' where they stole your letters. I ast her if she stole it, too, an' she says no. So I married Curley. Met him out to the Riverside Dance Palace that same night. You listenin'?

Well, I ain't told this to nobody before. Maybe I oughtn'n to. I don't like Curley. He ain't a nice fella.... Coulda been in the movies, an' had nice clothes -- all them nice clothes like they wear. An' I coulda sat in them big hotels, an' had pitchers took of me. When they had them previews I coulda went to them, an' spoke in the radio, an' it wouldn'ta cost me a cent because I was in the pitcher. An' all them nice clothes like they wear. Because this guy says I was a natural.

WRITING EVALUATION FORM - *Of Mice and Men*

Name _____ Date _____

Writing Assignment #1 for the *Of Mice and Men* unit   Grade _____

Circle One For Each Item:

Description (paragraph 1)	excellent	good	fair	poor
Plans (body paragraphs)	excellent	workable	fair	not realistic
Conclusion	excellent	good	fair	poor
Grammar:	excellent	good	fair	poor (errors noted)
Spelling:	excellent	good	fair	poor (errors noted)
Punctuation:	excellent	good	fair	poor (errors noted)
Legibility:	excellent	good	fair	poor

Strengths:

Weaknesses:

Comments/Suggestions:

LESSON EIGHT

Objectives
>   1. To give students time to complete their grammar evaluations and/or work on their writing assignment revisions
>   2. To give students a brief review of several commonly misused points of grammar

Activity #1

Give students some time at the beginning of this period to either complete their grammar exercises or to work on their writing assignment revisions. If some students have completed both of these projects, they should work on their nonfiction reading assignments.

Activity #2

Discuss the revision of the grammar exercise in detail. Have students point out the errors made in each sentence, and explain how and why the corrections should be made.

LESSON NINE

Objectives
>   1. To discuss the ideas and themes from *Of Mice and Men* in greater detail
>   2. To have students exercise their critical thinking skills
>   3. To try to relate some of the ideas in *Of Mice and Men* to the students' lives

Activity #1

Choose the questions from the Extra Discussion Questions/Writing Assignments which seem most appropriate for your students. A class discussion of these questions is most effective if students have been given the opportunity to formulate answers to the questions prior to the discussion. To this end, you may either have all the students formulate answers to all the questions, divide your class into groups and assign one or more questions to each group, or you could assign one question to each student in your class. The option you choose will make a difference in the amount of class time needed for this activity.

Activity #2

After students have had ample time to formulate answers to the questions, begin your class discussion of the questions and the ideas presented by the questions. Be sure students take notes during the discussion so they have information to study for the unit test.

EXTRA DISCUSSION QUESTIONS/WRITING ASSIGNMENTS
Of Mice and Men

Interpretive

1. From what point of view is the story told, and why is that important?

2. What is the setting, and what does it add to the story?

3. Are the characters in *Of Mice and Men* stereotypes? If so, explain the usefulness of employing stereotypes in the book. If they are not, explain how they merit individuality.

4. What are the main conflicts in the story, and how are they resolved?

5. What is foreshadowing? Give examples of foreshadowing used in *Of Mice and Men*.

6. Give a complete character analysis of George.

7. Based on the facts in the story, can you tell approximately in what year the story takes place? Does it matter?

8. Explain the role of each of these characters: Curley, Slim, Candy, Carlson, Crooks, and Curley's wife.

Critical

9. Explain the significance of the title "*Of Mice and Men*".

10. From almost the beginning of the story we know that Lennie is going to get into trouble. How do we know that, and how does Steinbeck hold our interest through the events of the story from that point to the climax?

11. Compare and contrast ranch life today with ranch life in the 1930's.

12. Why did the boss and Slim think it was odd that George and Lennie traveled around together? Would people think it odd today? Why or why not?

13. Compare and contrast Candy and Carlson.

14. Why did George kill Lennie?

15. Describe Steinbeck's writing style. How does it influence our perception of the story?

16. Give a rationale for the six divisions made in the story.

Of Mice and Men Extra Discussion Questions page 2

17. Who is the main character of the book? Defend your choice.

18. What universal themes are present in *Of Mice and Men*?

19. Where else could Lennie have gone besides with George? Was George wrong for taking Lennie with him? Would Lennie have been "better off" in an institution? Explain your answer.

Critical/Personal Response

20. Is the story of *Of Mice and Men* believable? Why or why not?

21. *Of Mice and Men* is a very short novel. could anything have been gained by including more scenes from the time before or after the events of the story? If so, what could have been added and for what purpose? If not, explain why not.

22. If you were George, what do you think you would have done about Lennie after he killed Curley's wife?

23. Who is responsible for Curley's wife's death? Defend your answer.

Personal Response

24. Suppose you had a friend who accidentally killed someone. Would you help him (or her)? What would you do?

25. If a homeless person would ask you for help, what could you do for him given your present limitations, whatever they may be (financial limitations, etc.)?

26. What is the value of having a good friend?

27. Would you have liked to have been a ranch hand like George? Explain why or why not.

Quotations

1. "Uh-uh. Jus' a dead mouse, George. I didn' kill it. Honest! I found it. I found it dead."

2. "God, you're a lot of trouble," said George. "I could get along so easy and so nice if I didn't have you on my tail. I could live so easy and maybe have a girl."

Of Mice and Men Extra Discussion Questions page 3

3. "They was so little," he said, apologetically. "I'd pet 'em, and pretty soon they bit my fingers and I pinched their heads a little and then they was dead--because they was so little."

4. "Well, I could. I could go off in the hills there. Some place I'd find a cave."

5. "No--look! I was jus' foolin', Lennie. 'Cause I want you to stay with me."

6. "With us it ain't like that. We got a future. We got somebody to talk to that gives a damn about us. We don't have to sit in no bar room blowin' our jack jus' because we got no place else to go."

7. "Well, I never seen one guy take so much trouble for another guy. I just like to know what your interest is."

8. He said ominously, "Well, he better watch out for Lennie."

9. Lennie cried out suddenly--"I don' like this place, George. This ain't no good place. I wanna get outa here."

10. "He's a nice fella," said Slim. "Guy don't need no sense to be a nice fella."

11. "Look, Candy. This ol' dog jus' suffers hisself all the time. If you was to take him out and shoot him right in the back of the head--" he leaned over and pointed, "--right there, why he'd never know what hit him."

12. "She's gonna make a mess. They's gonna be a bad mess about her. She's a jail bait all set on the trigger."

13. They looked at one another, amazed. This thing they had never really believed in was coming true.

14. "I ought to of shot that dog myself, George. I shouldn't ought to of let no stranger shoot my dog."

15. "Maybe you can see now. You got George. You *know* he's goin' to come back. S'pose you didn't have nobody. S'pose you couldn't go into the bunk house and play rummy 'cause you was black. How'd you like that?. . . A guy needs somebody--to be near him." He whined, "A guy goes nuts if he ain't got nobody. Don't make no difference who the guy is, long as he's with you. I tell ya," he cried, "I tell ya a guy gets too lonely an' he gets sick."

16. Nobody never gets to heaven, and nobody gets no land.

Of Mice and Men Extra Discussion Questions page 4

17. "Sure they all want it. Everybody wants a little bit of land, not much. Jus' som'thin' that was his."

18. "We ain't got nothing to say to you at all. We know what we got, and we don't care whether you know it or not."

19. "Maybe you guys better go," he said. "I ain't sure I want you in here no more. A colored man got to have some rights even if he don't like 'em."

20. "You guys comin' in an' settin' made me forget. What she says is true."

21. "God damn you," he cried. "Why do you got to get killed? You ain't so little as mice."

22. "I coulda made somethin' of myself." She said darkly, "Maybe I will yet."

23. For a moment he seemed bewildered. And then he whispered in fright, "I done a bad thing. I done another bad thing."

24. "What we gonna do now, George? What we gonna do now?"

25. "I guess we gotta get 'im an' lock 'im up. We can't let 'im get away. Why, the poor bastard'd starve."

26. "You an' me can get that little place, can't we, George? You an' me can go there an' live nice, can't we, George? Can't we?"

27. "--I think I knowed from the very first. I think I knowed we'd never do her. He usta like to hear about it so much I got tot thinking maybe we would."

28. Slim came directly to George and sat down beside him, sat very close to him. "Never you mind," said Slim. "A guy got to sometimes."

LESSON TEN

Objective
   To complete discussions begun in Lesson Nine

Activity
   Since part of Lesson Nine was taken up with giving students time to formulate answers, you will probably need a substantial portion of this class period to complete your class discussions.

NOTE: If your discussions finish early, you could give students the remainder of this class period to work on their class notes, the nonfiction reading assignment, or to give a little report about how your Project Homeless is going.

LESSON ELEVEN

Objectives
To review all of the vocabulary work done in this unit

Activity
Choose one (or more) of the vocabulary review activities listed on the next page(s) and spend your class period as directed in the activity. Some of the materials for these review activities are located in the Extra Activities Packet in this unit.

VOCABULARY REVIEW ACTIVITIES

1. Divide your class into two teams and have an old-fashioned spelling or definition bee.

2. Give each of your students (or students in groups of two, three or four) a *Of Mice and Men* Vocabulary Word Search Puzzle. The person (group) to find all of the vocabulary words in the puzzle first wins.

3. Give students a *Of Mice and Men* Vocabulary Word Search Puzzle without the word list. The person or group to find the most vocabulary words in the puzzle wins.

4. Use a *Of Mice and Men* Vocabulary Crossword Puzzle. Put the puzzle onto a transparency on the overhead projector (so everyone can see it), and do the puzzle together as a class.

5. Give students a *Of Mice and Men* Vocabulary Matching Worksheet to do.

6. Divide your class into two teams. Use the *Of Mice and Men* vocabulary words with their letters jumbled as a word list. Student 1 from Team A faces off against Student 1 from Team B. You write the first jumbled word on the board. The first student (1A or 1B) to unscramble the word wins the chance for his/her team to score points. If 1A wins the jumble, go to student 2A and give him/her a definition. He/she must give you the correct spelling of the vocabulary word which fits that definition. If he/she does, Team A scores a point, and you give student 3A a definition for which you expect a correctly spelled matching vocabulary word. Continue giving Team A definitions until some team member makes an incorrect response. An incorrect response sends the game back to the jumbled-word face off, this time with students 2A and 2B. Instead of repeating giving definitions to the first few students of each team, continue with the student after the one who gave the last incorrect response on the team. For example, if Team B wins the jumbled-word face-off, and student 5B gave the last incorrect answer for Team B, you would start this round of definition questions with student 6B, and so on. The team with the most points wins!

LESSON TWELVE

Objectives
    1. To give students the opportunity to practice writing to persuade
    2. To have students review the events of the novel and the traits of the main characters
    3. To give the teacher the opportunity to evaluate students' persuasive writing skills

Activity

    Distribute Writing Assignment #3 and discuss the directions in detail. Give students the remainder of the class time to work on this assignment.

LESSON THIRTEEN

Objectives
    1. To widen the breadth of students' knowledge about the topics discussed or touched upon in *Of Mice and Men*
    2. To check students' nonfiction reading assignments

Activity

    Ask each student to give a brief oral report about the nonfiction work he/she read for the nonfiction reading assignment. Your criteria for evaluating this report will vary depending on the level of your students. You may wish for students to give a complete report without using notes of any kind, or you may want students to read directly from a written report, or you may want to do something in between these two extremes. Just make students aware of your criteria in ample time for them to prepare their reports.

    Start with one student's report. After that, ask if anyone else in the class has read on a topic related to the first student's report. If no one has, choose another student at random. After each report, be sure to ask if anyone has a report related to the one just completed. That will help keep a continuity during the discussion of the reports.

WRITING ASSIGNMENT #3 - *Of Mice and Men*

PROMPT

Now that you have completed reading the novelette, you know that George kills Lennie. This act is presented as the humane thing to do for Lennie, which it very well could have been. Playing Devil's Advocate, though, one could ask if, indeed, this was the correct decision. If Lennie had been taken to trial, perhaps he would have been excused on grounds of lack of mental competence and may have been given a better life than he had had with George.

In this writing assignment, we're putting George on trial for murdering Lennie. You are to become either the attorney for George's defense or the prosecuting attorney. Your assignment is to write your closing arguments to the jury. (Closing arguments are a lawyers final summary of his case and his best efforts at persuading the jury to his side.)

PREWRITING

To begin, decide which side you want to take--George's defense or the prosecution. On a piece of paper, jot down the main points, the facts which will support your case. Decide which points are your strongest and which of the arguments you will make are weaker. Organize your points from weakest to strongest and jot down anything you can think of which will support or explain your points.

DRAFTING

Begin with an introductory paragraph in which you introduce the jury to your side of the case. Follow that with one paragraph for each of the main points you have to support your case. Fill in each paragraph with examples and facts which support your main point. Then, write a paragraph in which you make your final closing statements.

PROMPT

When you finish your rough draft, ask a student who sits near you to read it. After reading your rough draft, he/she should tell you what he/she liked best about your work, which parts were difficult to understand, and ways in which your work could be improved. Reread your paper considering your critic's comments and make the corrections you think are necessary.

PROOFREADING

Do a final proofreading of your paper double-checking your grammar, spelling, organization, and the clarity of your ideas.

LESSON FOURTEEN

Objective
  To review the main ideas presented in *Of Mice and Men*

Activity #1
  Choose one of the review games/activities included in the packet and spend your class period as outlined there. Some materials for these activities are located in the Unit Resource section of this unit.

Activity #2
  Remind students that the Unit Test will be in the next class meeting. Stress the review of the Study Guides and their class notes as a last minute, brush-up review for homework.

REVIEW GAMES/ACTIVITIES - *Of Mice and Men*

1. Ask the class to make up a unit test for *Of Mice and Men*. The test should have 4 sections: matching, true/false, short answer, and essay. Students may use 1/2 period to make the test and then swap papers and use the other 1/2 class period to take a test a classmate has devised. (open book) You may want to use the unit test included in this packet or take questions from the students' unit tests to formulate your own test.

2. Take 1/2 period for students to make up true and false questions (including the answers). Collect the papers and divide the class into two teams. Draw a big tic-tac-toe board on the chalk board. Make one team X and one team O. Ask questions to each side, giving each student one turn. If the question is answered correctly, that students' team's letter (X or O) is placed in the box. If the answer is incorrect, no mark is placed in the box. The object is to get three marks in a row like tic-tac-toe. You may want to keep track of the number of games won for each team.

3. Take 1/2 period for students to make up questions (true/false and short answer). Collect the questions. Divide the class into two teams. You'll alternate asking questions to individual members of teams A & B (like in a spelling bee). The question keeps going from A to B until it is correctly answered, then a new question is asked. A correct answer does not allow the team to get another question. Correct answers are +2 points; incorrect answers are -1 point.

4. Have students pair up and quiz each other from their study guides and class notes.

5. Give students a *Of Mice and Men* crossword puzzle to complete.

6. Divide your class into two teams. Use the *Of Mice and Men* crossword words with their letters jumbled as a word list. Student 1 from Team A faces off against Student 1 from Team B. You write the first jumbled word on the board. The first student (1A or 1B) to unscramble the word wins the chance for his/her team to score points. If 1A wins the jumble, go to student 2A and give him/her a clue. He/she must give you the correct word which matches that clue. If he/she does, Team A scores a point, and you give student 3A a clue for which you expect another correct response. Continue giving Team A clues until some team member makes an incorrect response. An incorrect response sends the game back to the jumbled-word face off, this time with students 2A and 2B. Instead of repeating giving clues to the first few students of each team, continue with the student after the one who gave the last incorrect response on the team. For example, if Team B wins the jumbled-word face-off, and student 5B gave the last incorrect answer for Team B, you would start this round of clue questions with student 6B, and so on.

UNIT TESTS

SHORT ANSWER UNIT TEST #1 - *Of Mice and Men*

I. Matching/Identify

___ 1. Slim   A. stable man

___ 2. George   B. killed Candy's dog

___ 3. Candy   C. foreman; reasonable; understands George & Lennie

___ 4. Lennie   D. ill-tempered son of the boss

___ 5. Crooks   E. kills Lennie

___ 6. Carlson   F. is killed by Lennie

___ 7. Curley   G. mentally slow, physically strong; likes soft things

___ 8. Curley's wife H. the old swamper

II. Short Answer

1. After George reprimands him, Lennie offers to go away and live in a cave. What is George's response?

2. Why are George and Lennie different from "other guys like us that work on ranches?"

3. What are George and Lennie going to do someday?

4. Slim and George have a long conversation. Slim says it's funny how George and Lennie go around together. What is George's answer?

Mice and Men Short Answer Unit Test 1 Page 2

5. What does Candy want when he hears about George's and Lennie's plan? What is he willing to contribute?

6. Why did Curley fight with Lennie? What happened?

7. Lennie tells Crooks about the land. What is his reply at first?

8. What happened to Lennie's puppy? What was his reaction?

9. Why did Lennie kill Curley's wife?

10. How and why did George kill Lennie?

Mice and Men Short Answer Unit Test 1 page 3

III. Essay

What do we learn from *Of Mice and Men*? Explain in detail using examples from the novel.

IV. Vocabulary

Listen to the vocabulary word and spell it.
After you have spelled all the words, go back and write down the definitions.

1.

2.

3.

4.

5.

6.

7.

8.

9.

10.

SHORT ANSWER UNIT TEST 2 - *Of Mice and Men*

I. Matching

___ 1. Slim   A. the old swamper

___ 2. George   B. stable man

___ 3. Candy   C. mentally slow; physically strong; liked soft things

___ 4. Lennie   D. killed Candy's dog

___ 5. Crooks   E. is killed by Lennie

___ 6. Carlson   F. foreman; reasonable; understands George & Lennie

___ 7. Curley   G. kills Lennie

___ 8. Curley's wife   H. ill-tempered son of the boss

Mice and Men Short Answer Unit Test 2 Page 2

II. Short Answer
1. What trouble did George and Lennie have in Weed?

2. Why are George and Lennie different from the other "guys like us that work on ranches"?

3. What are George and Lennie going to do someday?

4. Describe Curley's wife. What's the problem about her?

5. Why did Curley fight with Lennie? What happened?

6. What happened to Lennie's puppy? What is his reaction?

Mice and Men Short Answer Unit Test 2 Page 3

III. Quotations: Identify the speaker and explain the significance of these quotes:

1. "I don' like this place, George. This ain't no good place. I wanna get outa here."

2. "This ol' dog jus' suffers hisself all the time. If you was to take him out and shoot him right in the back of the head--" he leaned over and pointed, "--right there, why he'd never know what hit him."

3. "She's gonna make a mess. They's gonna be a bad mess about her. She's a jail bait all set on the trigger."

4. "I ought to of shot that dog myself, George. I shouldn't ought to of let no stranger shoot my dog."

5. Nobody never gets to heaven, and nobody gets no land.

6. "You guys comin' in an' settin' made me forget. What she says is true."

7. For a moment he seemed bewildered. And then he whispered in fright, "I done a bad thing. I done another bad thing."

8. "What we gonna do now, George? What we gonna do now?"

9. "Never you mind," [he said]. "A guy got to sometimes."

Mice and Men Short Answer Unit Test 2 page 4

IV. Vocabulary

    Listen to the vocabulary word and spell it.
    After you have spelled all the words, go back and write down the definitions.

1.

2.

3.

4.

5.

6.

7.

8.

9.

10.

KEY: SHORT ANSWER UNIT TESTS - *Of Mice and Men*

The short answer questions are taken directly from the study guides.
If you need to look up the answers, you will find them in the study guide section.

Answers to the composition questions will vary depending on your
class discussions and the level of your students.

For the vocabulary section of the test, choose ten of the
words from the vocabulary lists to read orally for your students.

The answers to the matching section of the test are below.

Answers to the matching section of the Advanced Short Answer Unit Test
are the same as for Short Answer Unit Test #2.

<u>Test #1</u>   <u>Test #2</u>
1. C   1. F
2. E   2. G
3. H   3. A
4. G   4. C
5. A   5. B
6. B   6. D
7. D   7. H
8. F   8. E

ADVANCED SHORT ANSWER UNIT TEST - *Of Mice and Men*

I. Matching

___ 1. Slim   A. the old swamper

___ 2. George   B. stable man

___ 3. Candy   C. mentally slow; physically strong; liked soft things

___ 4. Lennie   D. killed Candy's dog

___ 5. Crooks   E. is killed by Lennie

___ 6. Carlson   F. foreman; reasonable; understands George & Lennie

___ 7. Curley   G. kills Lennie

___ 8. Curley's wife   H. ill-tempered son of the boss

II. Short Answer

1. What is foreshadowing? Give 2 examples of foreshadowing in *Of Mice and Men*.

2. Give a complete character analysis of George.

Mice and Men Advanced Short Answer Unit Test Page 2

3. Why did Lennie have to die?

4. Who is the main character of the book? Explain your choice.

5. Who is responsible for Curley's wife's death? Explain your choice.

Mice and Men Advanced Short Answer Unit Test Page 3

III. Quotations: Explain the importance and meaning of the following quotations.

1. "God, you're a lot of trouble," said George. "I could get along so easy and so nice if I didn't have you on my tail. I could live so easy and maybe have a girl."

2. "I ought to of shot that dog myself, George. I shouldn't ought to of let no stranger shoot my dog."

3. "Nobody never gets to heaven, and nobody gets no land."

4. "God damn you," he cried. "Why do you got to get killed? You ain't so little as mice."

5. "I coulda made somethin' of myself." She said darkly, "Maybe I will yet."

6. "What we gonna do now, George? What we gonna do now?"

7. Slim came directly to George and sat down beside him, sat very close to him. "Never you mind," said Slim. "A guy got to sometimes."

Mice and Men Advanced Short Answer Unit Test Page 4

IV. Vocabulary

    Listen to the vocabulary words and write them down. After you have written down all the words, write a paragraph in which you use all the words. The paragraph must in some way relate to *Of Mice and Men*.

MULTIPLE CHOICE UNIT TEST 1 - *Of Mice and Men*

I. Matching

1. Slim   A. stable man

2. George   B. killed Candy's dog

3. Candy   C. foreman; reasonable; understands George & Lennie

4. Lennie   D. ill-tempered son of the boss

5. Crooks   E. kills Lennie

6. Carlson   F. is killed by Lennie

7. Curley   G. mentally slow, physically strong; likes soft things

8. Curley's wife   H. the old swamper

II. Multiple Choice

1. What trouble did George and Lennie have in Weed?
    a. They got drunk and rowdy.
    b. They did something & men came after them.
    c. They lost all their money playing cards.
    d. They got fired.

2. What does George say he could do if he were alone?
    a. go to a "cat house"
    b. drink whiskey all night
    c. play cards at a pool hall all night
    d. all of the above

3. Lennie offers to go away and live in a cave. What is George's response?
    a. He punches Lennie.
    b. He helps him pack his gear.
    c. He tells Lennie that he doesn't want him to go.
    d. none of the above

4. Why are George and Lennie different from the other "guys like [them] that work on ranches"?
    a. They are actually wealthy.
    b. They like their work and want to do it forever.
    c. They are not drifters.
    d. Each has the other to look out for him.

Mice and Men Multiple Choice Unit Test 1 page 2

5. What are George and Lennie going to do someday?
    a. have a little piece of land
    b. have some animals and crops
    c. live off the fat of the land
    d. all of the above

6. What does Slim have that Lennie wants?
    a. a gun
    b. puppies
    c. a wife
    d. the best bunk

7. What will Lennie's job be when he and George get their land?
    a. tend the rabbits
    b. milk the cow
    c. plow the fields
    d. cook

8. Why did Curley fight with Lennie?
    a. Curley thought Lennie was laughing at him.
    b. They both wanted the same puppy.
    c. Lennie punched him first.
    d. Lennie made a rude remark about Curley's wife.

9. What happened to Lennie's puppy?
    a. Lennie killed it.
    b. Carlson killed it.
    c. George killed it.
    d. It ran away.

10. What was George's reaction when he found out about Curley's wife's death?
    a. He was furious.
    b. He immediately ran after Lennie to yell at him.
    c. He was totally shocked.
    d. He tried to figure out how to best protect Lennie.

11. Would George ever get a piece of land?
    a. Yes, he and Candy were making plans together.
    b. Yes, he wanted to get the land for Lennie's sake.
    c. No, he never really wanted it anyway.
    d. No, he realized that it was just a dream that would never come true.

Mice and Men Multiple Choice Unit Test 1 page 3

III. Quotations: Identify the speaker:

A = Curley's wife   **B** = Lennie   **C** = Candy   **D** = George

E = Curley   **F** = Carlson   **G** = Crooks   **H** = Slim

1. "I don' like this place, George. This ain't no good place. I wanna get outa here."

2. "This ol' dog jus' suffers hisself all the time. If you was to take him out and shoot him right in the back of the head--" he leaned over and pointed, "--right there, why he'd never know what hit him."

3. "She's gonna make a mess. They's gonna be a bad mess about her. She's a jail bait all set on the trigger."

4. "I ought to of shot that dog myself, George. I shouldn't ought to of let no stranger shoot my dog."

5. "Nobody never gets to heaven, and nobody gets no land."

6. "You guys comin' in an' settin' made me forget. What she says is true."

7. For a moment he seemed bewildered. And then he whispered in fright, "I done a bad thing. I done another bad thing."

8. "What we gonna do now, George? What we gonna do now?"

9. "Never you mind," [he said]. "A guy got to sometimes."

Mice and Men Multiple Choice Unit Test 1 page 4

IV. Vocabulary (Matching)

1. derogatory
2. indignation
3. meager
4. subdued
5. bewildered
6. disarming
7. complacently
8. quivering
9. dejectedly
10. persuasive
11. anguished
12. ominously
13. confided
14. contemplated
15. morosely
16. skeptically
17. sniveled
18. gestured
19. ashamedly
20. reprehensible

A. considered thoughtfully
B. cried or wept with sniffling
C. to quiet or bring under control by physical force
D. showing an agonizing physical or mental pain
E. an anger aroused by something unjust, mean or unworthy
F. confused; befuddled
G. told private matters not intended to be publicly known
H. with foreboding
I. detracting or disparaging
J. trembling
K. endearing; tending to remove hostility or suspicion
L. glumly; gloomily
M. showing a feeling of guilt
N. sadly, depressed or disheartened
O. In a self-satisfied manner
P. made a motion to express a thought or to emphasize speech
Q. deficient in quantity; scant
R. showing doubt or disbelief; questioningly
S. convincing
T. worthy of blame; deserving censure

MULTIPLE CHOICE UNIT TEST 2 - *Of Mice and Men*

I. Matching

1. Slim   A. the old swamper

2. George   B. stable man

3. Candy   C. mentally slow; physically strong; liked soft things

4. Lennie   D. killed Candy's dog

5. Crooks   E. is killed by Lennie

6. Carlson   F. foreman; reasonable; understands George & Lennie

7. Curley   G. kills Lennie

8. Curley's wife   H. ill-tempered son of the boss

II. Multiple Choice

1. What trouble did George and Lennie have in Weed?
        a. They did something & men came after them.
        b. They got fired.
        c. They lost all their money playing cards.
        d. They got drunk and rowdy.

2. What does George say he could do if he were alone?
        a. live off the fat of the land
        b. drink whiskey all night
        c. have a steady job
        d. all of the above

3. Lennie offers to go away and live in a cave. What is George's response?
        a. He tells Lennie that he doesn't want him to go.
        b. He punches Lennie.
        c. He helps him pack his gear.
        d. none of the above

4. Why are George and Lennie different from the other "guys like [them] that work on ranches"?
        a. They like their work and want to do it forever.
        b. They are not drifters.
        c. Each has the other to look out for him.
        d. They are actually wealthy.

Mice and Men Multiple Choice Unit Test 2 page 2

5. What are George and Lennie going to do someday?
    a. have a little piece of land
    b. raise rabbits
    c. live off the fat of the land
    d. all of the above

6. What does Slim have that Lennie wants?
    a. a wife
    b. a gun
    c. puppies
    d. a rabbit

7. What will Lennie's job be when he and George get their land?
    a. plow the fields
    b. milk the cow
    c. tend the rabbits
    d. cook

8. Why did Curley fight with Lennie?
    a. Lennie punched him first.
    b. Curley thought Lennie was laughing at him.
    c. They both wanted the same puppy.
    d. Lennie made a rude remark about Curley's wife.

9. What happened to Lennie's puppy?
    a. George killed it.
    b. Carlson killed it.
    c. Lennie killed it.
    d. It ran away.

10. What was George's reaction when he found out about Curley's wife's death?
    a. He was furious.
    b. He tried to figure out how to best protect Lennie.
    c. He immediately ran after Lennie to yell at him.
    d. He was totally shocked.

11. Would George ever get a piece of land?
    a. No, he realized that it was just a dream that would never come true.
    b. Yes, he wanted to get the land for Lennie's sake.
    c. Yes, he and Candy were making plans together.
    d. No, he never really wanted it anyway.

Mice and Men Multiple Choice Unit Test 2 page 3

III. Quotations: Identify the speaker:

A = Slim **B** = George **C** = Candy **D** = Lennie

E = Crooks **F** = Carlson **G** = Curley **H** = Curley's wife

1. "I don' like this place, George. This ain't no good place. I wanna get outa here."

2. "This ol' dog jus' suffers hisself all the time. If you was to take him out and shoot him right in the back of the head--" he leaned over and pointed, "--right there, why he'd never know what hit him."

3. "She's gonna make a mess. They's gonna be a bad mess about her. She's a jail bait all set on the trigger."

4. "I ought to of shot that dog myself, George. I shouldn't ought to of let no stranger shoot my dog."

5. "Nobody never gets to heaven, and nobody gets no land."

6. "You guys comin' in an' settin' made me forget. What she says is true."

7. For a moment he seemed bewildered. And then he whispered in fright, "I done a bad thing. I done another bad thing."

8. "What we gonna do now, George? What we gonna do now?"

9. "Never you mind," [he said]. "A guy got to sometimes."

Mice and Men Multiple Choice Unit Test 2 page 4

IV. Vocabulary (Matching)

1. bewildered	A. with a feeling of contempt; scornfully
2. appraised	B. deficient in quantity; scant
3. entranced	C. comforted
4. skeptically	D. showing doubt or disbelief; questioningly
5. sniveled	E. an anger aroused by something unjust, mean or unworthy
6. mauled	F. mournfully; sorrowfully
7. subdued	G. twisted or strained out of shape
8. plaintively	H. cried or wept with sniffling
9. apprehensive	I. to quiet or bring under control by physical force
10. contemptuously	J. made a motion to express a thought or to emphasize speech
11. belligerently	K. gloomily
12. contorted	L. hostilely, aggressively
13. gestured	M. confused; befuddled
14. sulkily	N. evaluated
15. subsided	O. uneasy; anxious
16. indignation	P. fascinated
17. consoled	Q. handled roughly; beaten up
18. meager	R. pacified; calmed
19. mollified	S. acting that consists mostly of gesture, no speech
20. pantomime	T. settled down

ANSWER SHEET - *Of Mice and Men*
Multiple Choice Unit Tests

I. Matching	II. Multiple Choice	III. Quotes	IV. Vocabulary
1. ___	1. ___	1. ___	1. ___
2. ___	2. ___	2. ___	2. ___
3. ___	3. ___	3. ___	3. ___
4. ___	4. ___	4. ___	4. ___
5. ___	5. ___	5. ___	5. ___
6. ___	6. ___	6. ___	6. ___
7. ___	7. ___	7. ___	7. ___
8. ___	8. ___	8. ___	8. ___
	9. ___	9. ___	9. ___
	10. ___		10. ___
	11. ___		11. ___
			12. ___
			13. ___
			14. ___
			15. ___
			16. ___
			17. ___
			18. ___
			19. ___
			20. ___

ANSWER SHEET KEY - *Of Mice and Men*
Multiple Choice Unit Tests

Test 1 answers are in the left hand column. Test 2 answers are in the right hand column.

MATCHING	MULTIPLE CHOICE	QUOTES	VOCABULARY
1. C F	1. B A	1. B D	1. I M
2. E G	2. D D	2. F F	2. E N
3. H A	3. C A	3. D B	3. Q P
4. G C	4. D C	4. C C	4. C D
5. A B	5. D D	5. G E	5. F H
6. B D	6. B C	6. G E	6. K Q
7. D H	7. A C	7. B D	7. O I
8. F E	8. A B	8. C C	8. J F
	9. A C	9. H A	9. N O
	10. D B		10. S A
	11. D A		11. D L
			12. H G
			13. G J
			14. A K
			15. L T
			16. R E
			17. B C
			18. P B
			19. M R
			20. T S

UNIT RESOURCE MATERIALS

BULLETIN BOARD IDEAS - *Of Mice and Men*

1. Save a space for students' best writing. Make a nice border. Cut out letters THE BEST or YOU'RE THE TOPS! with a cut-out top hat -- whatever title you want to show the meaning of the space. Staple up the best writing samples (or quizzes or whatever you have graded) on colorful paper.

2. Bring in (or have students bring in) pictures of farm life from magazines. Make a collage if you have enough different pictures (or post individual pictures on colorful paper if you only have a few pictures). This could also be a fun introductory activity if students participate. You could have the border and title done for the bulletin board and invite students to staple up their own pictures wherever they want them. It will only take a few minutes of class time, but the students will enjoy it and you can get your bulletin board done in a hurry.

3. Draw one of the word search puzzles onto the bulletin board. (Be sure to enlarge it.) Write the key words to one side. Invite students to take their pens or markers and find the words before and/or after class (or perhaps this could be an activity for students who finish their work early).

4. Use cut-out pictures of people who appear to be friends. Contrast them with people who appear to be lonely. Title the board OF MICE AND MEN: A STORY OF FRIENDSHIP AND LONELINESS.

5. See the introductory activity in Lesson One.

6. Do a bulletin board about loneliness and use it as a springboard for discussion. For example, put up pictures of people who look lonely. Have students look at the pictures and, considering any clues given in the pictures, offer suggestions as to how each person might become less lonely.

7. Do a bulletin board about careers available in agriculture or working with handicapped people.

8. If you decide to do Project Homeless in conjunction with this unit, make a bulletin board on which you can keep your activity updates.

EXTRA ACTIVITIES

One of the difficulties in teaching a novel is that all students don't read at the same speed. One student who likes to read may take the book home and finish it in a day or two. Sometimes a few students finish the in-class assignments early. The problem, then, is finding suitable extra activities for students.

The best thing I've found is to keep a little library in the classroom. For this unit on *Of Mice and Men*, you might check out from the school library other books by Steinbeck. A biography of the author would be interesting for some students. You may include other related books and articles about farm and ranch life, physically and mentally handicapped persons in our society (and how we treat them), life among the working homeless or elderly in today's world, etc.

Other things you may keep on hand are puzzles. We have made some relating directly to *Of Mice and Men* for you. Feel free to duplicate them for your class.

Some students may like to draw. You might devise a contest or allow some extra-credit grade for students who draw characters or scenes from *Of Mice and Men*. Note, too, that if the students do not want to keep their drawings you may pick up some extra bulletin board materials this way. If you have a contest and you supply the prize (a CD or something like that perhaps), you could, possibly, make the drawing itself a non-refundable entry fee.

The pages which follow contain games, puzzles and worksheets. The keys, when appropriate, immediately follow the puzzle or worksheet. There are two main groups of activities: one group for the unit; that is, generally relating to the *Mice and Men* text, and another group of activities related strictly to the *Mice and Men* vocabulary.

Directions for the games, puzzles and worksheets are self-explanatory. The object here is to provide you with extra materials you may use in any way you choose.

MORE ACTIVITIES - *Of Mice and Men*

1. Pick a chapter or scene with a great deal of dialogue and have the students act it out on a stage. (Perhaps you could assign various scenes to different groups of students so more than one scene could be acted and more students could participate.)

2. Show a film version of *Of Mice and Men* to the class after you have completed reading the novel. Have students evaluate the movie and compare/contrast it with the book. If the students have tried writing a chapter into a scene in a play, you may wish to discuss how the problems they encountered in changing the form were handled in the movie.

3. Have students design a book cover (front and back and inside flaps) for *Of Mice and Men*.

4. Have students design a bulletin board (ready to be put up; not just sketched) for *Of Mice and Men*.

5. Have a guest speaker discuss current farming techniques and problems.

6. Use some of the related topics (noted earlier for an in-class library) as topics for research, reports or written papers, or as topics for guest speakers.

7. Research what careers are currently available for slow but physically able people like Lennie.

8. If your school permits it, have a couple of caged mice (or hamsters) as pets in your classroom during this unit.

9. In conjunction with Writing Assignment #3 hold a complete trial for George. Have students work out all the parts for the witnesses, the judge and the attorney.

10. Have students write:
    a. Lennie's obituary
    b. a newspaper account of Lennie's death
    c. a poem or song with lyrics about Lennie
    d. one section of the book as a play

11. Other writing assignments:
    a. Suppose George is in a bunkhouse a few years after the action of our story takes place telling a friend about the events of this story. What do you think he would say?
    b. If you were writing the story today, what setting would you use for the two friends to carry out the same basic plot? Explain why.

12. Hold a discussion/workshop, the topic of which is "How to make and keep friends and still maintain your individuality."

WORD SEARCH - *Of Mice and Men*

All the words in this list are associated with *Of Mice and Men*. The words are placed backwards, forward, diagonally, up and down. The included words are listed below the word search.

```
Y M S L X R L D S L V B W G L Z S L B X N V Q G
K H H M W Y D K B T F M X Q J M P M N P W Y C T
F K X Z K K R S V Z E F W K L S J U M N P N B K
P R W Z N R C N Y M F I D G Q E Y T P P H R G Z
F E I Y B T B D X J O T N N G C N N S P W L H Z
T M R E B R L E N L F U O B X X C N Y D I N M Y
K R X I N L L P A A B T S G E A N S I Y N E X K
M C A B A D E E W N L U G E R C U R L E Y A S Q
L F Q M N T S Q R I S W G L A O K S V I R Q H M
L R S I P L I A M P R R S M L K F A F A M D S S
L R B Z S X B L T S O O P Q J B C F L L S V V P
C R O O K S X S O E N S N E C K P C L T X G B M
T A P K W N S W G S I K T Y Q Z T J I M L K W W
W R N D K O U Y B T L N X G N W V B Y H V L K B
M D L B B R B E Q X D D L G L B C B W K R V Q
K G V R Y S A L I N A S W Q C A F I G H T T K S
K F D S J D Q Y V M V N D H R G R P N Q M P C Q
```

BAD	CAVE	LAND	SALINAS
BARN	CLARA	LENNIE	SLIM
BEANS	CROOKS	LUGER	SMALL
BINDLE	CURLEY	MILTON	SOLITAIRE
BOSS	FIGHT	MOUSE	STEINBECK
BUNK	FORGOT	NECK	TRAMP
CAMPSITE	FRIENDS	PET	WEED
CANDY	GEORGE	PUPPIES	
CARLSON	HAND	RABBITS	

CROSSWORD - *Of Mice and Men*

Across
2. Curley's wife acts like one
6. Not good
8. Card game George plays
9. Ranch foreman
13. Ranch hand's bed
14. Lennie offers to go away & live in one
15. Old swamper whose dog was killed
16. Lennie was shot with it
17. One in charge
18. Lennie breaks Curley's wife's
19. Author

Down
1. Killed Candy's dog
3. What Lennie wants to tend someday
4. What Slim has that Lennie wants
5. Lennie carried a dead one in his pocket
7. He killed Lennie
10. He is mentally slow but physically strong
11. Ill-tempered son of the ranch owner
12. Outdoor place ranchers stay overnight
15. Stable man
17. Place to keep animals & store hay

CROSSWORD ANSWER KEY - *Of Mice and Men*

Across/Down answers as filled in the grid:

- BAD
- CARLSON
- TRABBCTC
- TRAMP
- MOUSE
- SOLITAIRE
- SLIM
- CURLEY
- BUNK
- CAVE
- CANDY
- LUGER
- CROOKS
- BOSS
- CANDY
- MCMPSIT
- NECK
- STEINBECK
- GEORGE

MATCHING QUIZ/WORKSHEET 1 - *Of Mice and Men*

___ 1. George   A. What George and Lennie hope to own someday

___ 2. Land   B. Lennie crushed Curley's

___ 3. Slim   C. Stable man

___ 4. Solitaire   D. Town George and Lennie had to leave

___ 5. Weed   E. Card game George plays

___ 6. Tramp   F. Not good

___ 7. Steinbeck   G. Lennie often did this; didn't remember

___ 8. Crooks   H. Lennie was shot with it

___ 9. Bindle   I. He killed Lennie

___ 10. Mouse   J. Ranch hand's bed

___ 11. Luger   K. Author

___ 12. Bad   L. Curley's wife acts like one

___ 13. Campsite   M. Outdoor place ranchers stay overnight

___ 14. Clara   N. Slang for a ranch hand's bedroll

___ 15. Curley   O. What Lennie liked to do to the dead mouse

___ 16. Hand   P. Lennie's aunt who gave him mice

___ 17. Bunk   Q. Lennie carried a dead one in his pocket

___ 18. Lennie   R. Ranch foreman

___ 19. Forgot   S. Ill-tempered son of the ranch owner

___ 20. Pet   T. He is mentally slow but physically strong

MATCHING QUIZ/WORKSHEET 2 - *Of Mice and Men*

___ 1. Carlson   A. George's last name

___ 2. Milton   B. One in charge

___ 3. Fight   C. Lennie breaks Curley's wife's

___ 4. Salinas   D. A few miles south of Soledad this river runs deep and green

___ 5. Tramp   E. Ranch foreman

___ 6. Forgot   F. Old swamper whose dog was killed

___ 7. Curley   G. Lennie often did this; didn't remember

___ 8. Weed   H. Town George and Lennie had to leave

___ 9. Puppies   I. Lennie's last name

___ 10. Candy   J. What Slim has that Lennie wants

___ 11. Barn   K. What Curley likes to do

___ 12. Rabbits   L. Place to keep animals and store hay

___ 13. Boss   M. Not good

___ 14. Slim   N. Killed Candy's dog

___ 15. Small   O. What Lennie wants to tend someday

___ 16. Pet   P. What Lennie liked to do to the dead mouse

___ 17. George   Q. Curley's wife acts like one

___ 18. Neck   R. Lennie carried a dead one in his pocket

___ 19. Bad   S. Ill-tempered son of the ranch owner

___ 20. Mouse   T. He killed Lennie

KEY: MATCHING QUIZ/WORKSHEETS - *Of Mice and Men*

Worksheet 1	Worksheet 2
1. I	1. N
2. A	2. A
3. R	3. K
4. E	4. D
5. D	5. Q
6. L	6. G
7. K	7. S
8. C	8. H
9. N	9. J
10. Q	10. F
11. H	11. L
12. F	12. O
13. M	13. B
14. P	14. E
15. S	15. O
16. B	16. P
17. J	17. T
18. T	18. C
19. G	19. M
20. O	20. R

JUGGLE LETTER REVIEW GAME CLUE SHEET - *Of Mice and Men*

SCRAMBLED	WORD	CLUE
PTRAM	TRAMP	Curley's wife acts like one
LCARONS	CARLSON	Killed Candy's dog
DNYAC	CANDY	Old swamper
VCEA	CAVE	Lennie offers to go away and live in one
IMLS	SLIM	Reasonable ranch foreman
NLNEEI	LENNIE	He's mentally slow but physically strong
IFNSRED	FRIENDS	George and Lennie, for example
NHDA	HAND	Lennie crushed Curley's
NRBA	BARN	Place to keep animals and store hay
TPE	PET	What Lennie liked to do to soft things
OFORTG	FORGOT	Lennie often did this; didn't remember
DEEW	WEED	Town George and Lennie had to leave
ISTCEKBNE	STEINBECK	Author
PSPUPIE	PUPPIES	What Slim had that Lennie wanted
GOEGRE	GEORGE	Killed Lennie
GHFTI	FIGHT	What Curley likes to do
IRITASLEO	SOLITAIRE	George's card game
ACRAL	CLARA	Lennie's aunt
ULERG	LUGER	George shot Lennie with it
IBTRBSA	RABBITS	What Lennie wants to tend someday
PSEMTCIA	CAMPSITE	Outdoor place ranchers stay overnight
ADB	BAD	Not good
UNKB	BUNK	Ranch hand's bed
OSSB	BOSS	One in charge
OKROSC	CROOKS	The stable man
ASNASLI	SALINAS	A few miles south of Soledad, this river runs deep
NOTLIM	MILTON	George's last name
ELCYUR	CURLEY	Ill-tempered son of the ranch owner
NLIBED	BINDLE	Slang for ranch hand's bedroll
ALDN	LAND	What George and Lennie hoped to own someday
CNKE	NECK	Lennie broke Curley's wife's
ALLMS	SMALL	Lennie's last name

VOCABULARY RESOURCE MATERIALS

VOCABULARY WORD SEARCH - *Of Mice and Men*

All the words in this list are associated with *Of Mice and Men* with emphasis on the vocabulary words being studied in the unit. The words are placed backwards, forward, diagonally, up and down. The included words are listed below the word search.

```
C D R P B D D D B Y G Y Y D I S A R M I N G L L
Y O C E R S X E E M L N L H Y M N D S V F W J R
M O N O T O N O U S K E P T I C A L L Y H N E R
N Q B C Q O F I U D I A S L N G O U Y Y D G T J
A J U G E K R O V Z B A P O A E G N L S A C G B
X N R I P A N T U E I U R P R I C T S E M P J T
D Y G C V I L D E N L J S P R O N A M O D C M P
W E K U M E E I D D D E R W P E M T L J L N T X
B J C O I R R I N D M E D G R A H L I P T E N P
N E N N U S G I E G C K N E Q D I E D V M C D S
Z R M T A N H T N E Y I G D E F D E N Y E O Z J
F S S U A R R E D G K I S D I E D M L S W L C G
B E X T S O T E D C L L I E H I R I G K I T Y G
G F I P T E B N I L B S D T F W K Y C W R V X H
Y O B N T P D M E P B G I N Y L K S F C G F E R
N W O Y M Z I B Z U M R O Q U A S H A M E D L Y
Y C P T L M G J S L W C Z S P A N T O M I M E P
```

ANGUISHED	CONSOLED	MOLLIFIED	RETORTED
APPRAISED	CONTORTED	MONOTONOUS	SKEPTICALLY
APPREHENSIVE	DISARMING	MOROSELY	SNIVELED
ASHAMEDLY	ENTRANCED	OMINOUSLY	SUBDUED
BELLIGERENTLY	GESTURED	PANTOMIME	SUBSIDED
BEMUSED	INDIGNATION	PLAINTIVELY	SULKILY
COMPLACENTLY	MAULED	PRECEDE	WRITHED
CONCEALING	MEAGER	PROFOUND	
CONFIDED	MIMICKING	QUIVERING	

VOCABULARY CROSSWORD - *Of Mice and Men*

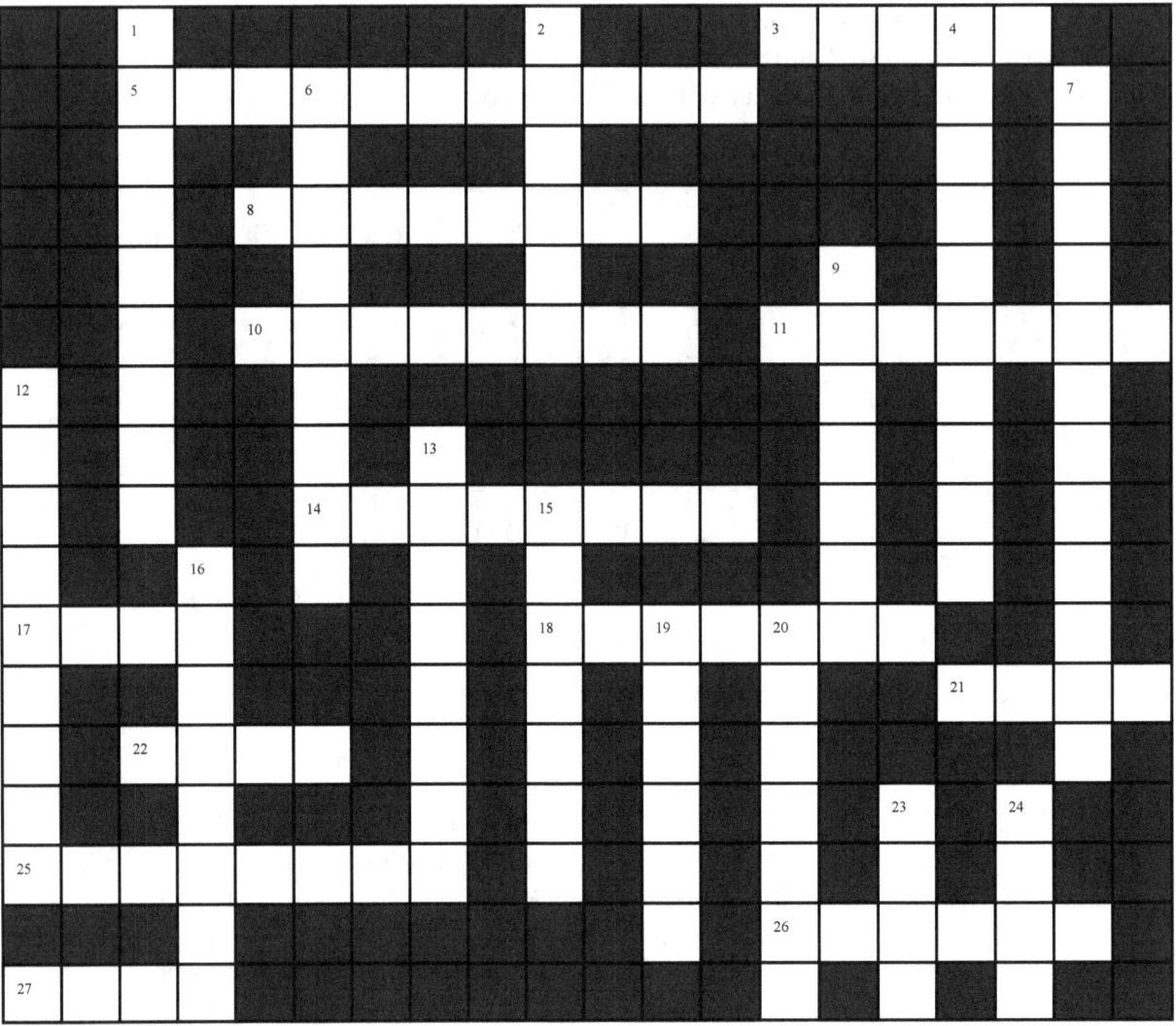

Across
- 3. Old swamper whose dog was killed
- 5. Showing doubt or disbelief
- 8. Cried or wept with sniffling
- 10. Told private matters not intended to be publicly known
- 11. Twisted
- 14. Glumly; gloomily
- 17. Lennie offers to go away & live in one
- 18. Put into deep thought
- 21. Town George and Lennie had to leave
- 22. One in charge
- 25. Made a motion to express a thought or emphasize speech
- 27. Lennie crushed Curley's

Down
- 1. Showing a feeling of guilt
- 2. Handled roughly; beaten up
- 4. Sadly, depressed or disheartened
- 6. Acting consisting mostly of gesture, no speech
- 7. Considered thoughtfully
- 9. Go before
- 12. Imitating
- 13. Complete; coming from the depths of one's being
- 15. To quiet or bring under control by physical force
- 16. Sharply replied
- 19. Deficient in quantity; scant
- 20. Gloomily
- 23. What George and Lennie hope to own someday
- 24. Ranch foreman

VOCABULARY CROSSWORD ANSWER KEY - *Of Mice and Men*

VOCABULARY WORKSHEET 1 - *Of Mice and Men*

___ 1. Morosely   A. Considered thoughtfully

___ 2. Confided   B. Gloomily

___ 3. Writhed   C. Mournfully; sorrowfully

___ 4. Complacently   D. Showing an agonizing physical or mental pain

___ 5. Concealing   E. Confused; befuddled

___ 6. Retorted   F. Pacified; calmed

___ 7. Monotonous   G. Handled roughly; beaten up

___ 8. Anguished   H. Unwillingly; hesitantly

___ 9. Entranced   I. Unvarying the vocal tone or pitch

___ 10. Consoled   J. Hiding

___ 11. Mollified   K. Evaluated

___ 12. Plaintively   L. Fascinated

___ 13. Quivering   M. Sharply replied

___ 14. Sulkily   N. Told private matters

___ 15. Mauled   O. In a self-satisfied manner

___ 16. Appraised   P. Trembling

___ 17. Contemplated   Q. Settled down

___ 18. Bewildered   R. Glumly; gloomily

___ 19. Subsided   S. Twisted

___ 20. Reluctantly   T. Comforted

VOCABULARY WORKSHEET 2 - *Of Mice and Men*

___ 1. Ominously   A. Showing a feeling of guilt

___ 2. Ashamedly   B. Twisted

___ 3. Apprehensive   C. Considered thoughtfully

___ 4. Concealing   D. To quiet or control by physical force

___ 5. Retorted   E. Hiding

___ 6. Skeptically   F. Unwillingly; hesitantly

___ 7. Complacently   G. Glumly; gloomily

___ 8. Morosely   H. Detracting or disparaging

___ 9. Profound   I. Showing doubt or disbelief; questioningly

___ 10. Disarming   J. In a self-satisfied manner

___ 11. Writhed   K. With foreboding

___ 12. Consoled   L. Comforted

___ 13. Mimicking   M. Uneasy; anxious

___ 14. Pantomime   N. Acting that consists mostly of gesture, no speech

___ 15. Contemplated   O. Imitating

___ 16. Impressively   P. Commanding attention; making a strong impression

___ 17. Derogatory   Q. Pacified; calmed

___ 18. Reluctantly   R. Endearing; tending to remove hostility

___ 19. Mollified   S. Sharply replied

___ 20. Subdued   T. Complete; coming from the depths of one's being

KEY: VOCABULARY WORKSHEETS - *Of Mice and Men*

Worksheet 1	Worksheet 2
1. R	1. K
2. N	2. A
3. S	3. M
4. O	4. E
5. J	5. S
6. M	6. I
7. I	7. J
8. D	8. G
9. L	9. T
10. T	10. R
11. F	11. B
12. C	12. L
13. P	13. O
14. B	14. N
15. G	15. C
16. K	16. P
17. A	17. H
18. E	18. F
19. Q	19. Q
20. H	20. D

VOCABULARY JUGGLE LETTER REVIEW GAME CLUES - *Of Mice and Men*

SCRAMBLED	WORD	CLUE
DNETECANR	ENTRANCED	Fascinated
USEIRSAVPE	PERSUASIVE	Convincing
HMLASDYAE	ASHAMEDLY	Showing a feeling of guilt
ILECAOGCNN	CONCEALING	Hiding
UDSENHAIG	ANGUISHED	Showing an agonizing physical or mental pain
ODPNORFU	PROFOUND	Complete; coming from the depths of one's being
OUTEONLSYUPMCT	CONTEMPTUOUSLY	Scornfully
CLRNLETUYAT	RELUCTANTLY	Unwillingly; hesitantly
INGSAIMRD	DISARMING	Endearing
EREBDWLIDE	BEWILDERED	Confused; befuddled
NEOOLDCS	CONSOLED	Comforted
MNCGKIMII	MIMICKING	Imitating
RVIINEGUQ	QUIVERING	Trembling
TPKYECALSLI	SKEPTICALLY	Showing doubt or disbelief
ISMEPLYIRSEV	IMPRESSIVELY	Commanding attention
UDRESETG	GESTURED	Motioned to express a thought or emphasize speech
DECOTTRNO	CONTORTED	Twisted or strained out of shape
ICDOFEND	CONFIDED	Told private matters
TNPLMTEAEDOC	CONTEMPLATED	Considered thoughtfully
EYOOLSMR	MOROSELY	Glumly; gloomily
BEDUDUS	SUBDUED	To quiet by physical force
LNSEUSLSEN	SULLENNESS	Gloominess
ETDIRWH	WRITHED	Twisted
VHSEEPAINEPR	APPREHENSIVE	Uneasy; anxious
ROEDOGRAYT	DEROGATORY	Detracting or disparaging
ULKLSYI	SULKILY	Gloomily
LDYEEETJCD	DEJECTEDLY	Sadly; depressed or disheartened
MTCLPCALYNEO	COMPLACENTLY	In a self-satisfied manner
TTEEODRR	RETORTED	Sharply replied
GEREMA	MEAGER	Deficient in quantity; scant
REEDCPE	PRECEDE	Go before
EISUDDBS	SUBSIDED	Settled down
EESDLVIN	SNIVELED	Cried or wept with sniffling
YNOLUOMSI	OMINOUSLY	With foreboding
YLNVEITIPLA	PLAINTIVELY	Mournfully; sorrowfully
TEAPMMNIO	PANTOMIME	Acting with gesture; no speech
EEEINRLBPRESH	REPREHENSIBLE	Worthy of blame